THE TWO INTELLECTUAL WORLDS

OF JOHN LOCKE

THE TWO INTELLECTUAL WORLDS OF JOHN LOCKE

Man, Person, and Spirits in the *Essay*

JOHN W. YOLTON

CORNELL UNIVERSITY PRESS
ITHACA & LONDON

Copyright © 2004 by Cornell University

All rights reserved. Except for brief quotations in a review, this book, or parts thereof, must not be reproduced in any form without permission in writing from the publisher. For information, address Cornell University Press, Sage House, 512 East State Street, Ithaca, New York 14850.

First published 2004 by Cornell University Press

Printed in the United States of America

Library of Congress Cataloging-in-Publication Data

Yolton, John W.
  The two intellectual worlds of John Locke : man, person, and spirits in the Essay / John W. Yolton.
      p. cm.
  Includes bibliographical references and index.
  ISBN 0-8014-4290-7 (cloth : alk. paper)
    1. Locke, John, 1632–1704. Essay concerning human understanding. 2. Knowledge, Theory of—History—17th century. I. Title.
  B1294.Y66 2004
  121—dc22
                                                                2004010282

Cornell University Press strives to use environmentally responsible suppliers and materials to the fullest extent possible in the publishing of its books. Such materials include vegetable-based, low-VOC inks and acid-free papers that are recycled, totally chlorine-free, or partly composed of nonwood fibers. For further information, visit our website at www.cornellpress.cornell.edu.

Cloth printing   10 9 8 7 6 5 4 3 2 1

Say first, of God above, or man below,
What can we reason, but from what we know?
Of man, what see we but his station here,
From which to reason, or to which refer?
Through worlds unnumbered, though the God be known,
'Tis ours to trace Him only in our own.
He, who through vast immensity can pierce,
See worlds on worlds compose one universe,
Observe how system into system runs,
What other planets circle other suns,
What varied being peoples every star,
May tell why Heaven has made us as we are.
But of this frame the bearings and the ties,
The strong connections, nice dependencies,
Gradations just, has thy pervading soul
Look'd through? or can a part contain the whole?

ALEXANDER POPE, *Essay on Man*, Epistle I

CONTENTS

Acknowledgments	xi
Locke Texts Cited	xiii
Introduction	1

CHAPTER 1. LOCKE'S MAN	9
1. Body-Mind, Man-Person	10
2. Action and Agency	14
3. Secular Self, Moral Self	18
3.1 On Being Self to Self	18
3.2 Person and Self	20
3.3 Self-Concern	23
4. Physical Man, Rational Man, Moral Man	23
5. Definitions of Man	25
6. The Fundamental Constitution of Man	27
6.1 The Constitution of Children	29
6.2 Rational Creatures	31
6.3 Definition and Theory	32
7. Man as Proprietor	34
Conclusion	36

CHAPTER 2. THE UNIVERSE AND OUR WORLD	38
1. The Universe	40

2. The Intellectual World as our World	45
2.1 Natural Philosophy as Speculation	46
2.2 Conjecture as Method	47
2.3 Examples of Natural Philosophy	54
2.4 Immaterial Principles and Immaterial Powers	58
3. A Second Intellectual World	59
Conclusion	62
CHAPTER 3. THE WORLD OF GOD, ANGELS, AND SPIRITS	64
1. Creatures, Beings and Spirits	65
1.1 Creatures	65
1.2 Beings	68
1.3 Spirits and Angels	70
2. Locke's Extravagant Conjecture	74
3. Two Properties of that World	77
3.1 Perfection	77
3.3.1 Happiness: The Happy God	79
3.3.2 Happiness: The Chief End of Man	82
Conclusion	86
CHAPTER 4. SPIRITS AND OUR IDEAS OF THEM	90
1. Ideas of Spirits	91
1.1 The Operation of Enlarging Ideas	93
1.2 Some Limitations	95
2. Conceivable, Intelligible	98
2.1 The Impossible	101
2.2 The Cannot	102
2.3 The Hard to Conceive	104
3. Two Other Accounts of Spirits	105
3.1 Burthogge	106
3.2 Bekker	108
Conclusion	112
CHAPTER 5. SOULS THAT BECOME SPIRITS	114
1. Soul as Spirit	117
2. The Relation of Man, Soul, and Body	121
2.1 Sameness of Man	122
2.2 Sameness of Spirit	126

3. Immortality and Bodily Shape	130
Conclusion	134
CHAPTER 6. GENERAL CONCLUSION	136
Notes	153
Bibliography	173
Index	175

ACKNOWLEDGMENTS

Chapter 1 is a slightly revised and expanded version of a paper published in the *Journal of the History of Ideas* in 2001 under that title. The rest of this study appears here for the first time.

I am indebted to John Higgins-Biddle and James G. Buickerood, both of whom took time out of their busy schedules to read an earlier version. Their critical questions and comments, as well as their encouragement, have led to a number of improvements. They also gathered information and articles for me on that curious figure Balthasar Bekker and his *Le Monde enchanté*. Before I was able to obtain a copy of this four-volume book on spirits, these two scholar-friends were able to examine copies of it for me. John Higgins-Biddle examined the Yale University Library copy, and James Buickerood was able to consult Locke's copy in the Locke Room at the Bodleian Library, Oxford. I also thank Rachel Lee of Rachel Lee Rare Books (Bristol) for finding a copy for me. Discussions with John Rogers about a number of terms and concepts in some of the chapters were very helpful.

I am especially grateful to my wife for copyediting the typescript. With her critical eye for sentences that are unclear and phrases that are awkward in expression, she has played her usual helpful role in improving the exposition.

J.W.Y.

LOCKE TEXTS CITED

Essay concerning Human Understanding. Edited by Peter H. Nidditch. Clarendon Edition of the Works of John Locke. Oxford: Clarendon Press, 1975. Cited as *Essay.*

Essays on the Law of Nature. Edited by W. von Leyden. Oxford: Clarendon Press, 1954. Cited as *Essays.*

A Paraphrase and Notes on the Epistles of St. Paul. 2 vols. Edited by Arthur W. Wainwright. Clarendon Edition of the Works of John Locke. Oxford: Clarendon Press, 1987.

Posthumous Works of John Locke. London: A. & J. Churchill, 1706. Contains:
  "Of the Conduct of the Understanding." Cited as "Conduct."
  "An Examination of P. Malebranche's Opinion of Seeing All Things in God."
  "A Discourse of Miracles."
  "Part of a Fourth Letter for Toleration, etc."

The Reasonableness of Christianity. Edited by John Higgins-Biddle. Clarendon Edition of the Works of John Locke. Oxford: Clarendon Press, 1999. Cited as *Reasonableness.*

Some Thoughts concerning Education. Edited by John W. Yolton and Jean S. Yolton. Clarendon Edition of the Works of John Locke. Oxford: Clarendon Press, 1989. Cited as *Education.*

Two Treatises of Government. Edited by Peter Laslett. Cambridge: Cambridge University Press, 1960; 2nd ed., 1971.

The Correspondence of John Locke. Vol. 4. Edited by E. S. De Beer. Clarendon Edition of the Works of John Locke. Oxford: Clarendon Press, 1979.

THE TWO INTELLECTUAL WORLDS

OF JOHN LOCKE

INTRODUCTION

In the chapters that follow, I offer a reading of John Locke's *An Essay concerning Human Understanding* that locates man, human beings, in the universe at large, a universe of other creatures and beings inhabiting material and spiritual domains. While the *Essay* is about human understanding, it is also an essay on man. Man is both a physical and rational Being, an actor in the material and social worlds, and a moral Being striving to live in a way that earns him a place in the next life. Locke's account of the extent and limits of knowledge is tempered by his concern for immortality and just life.

In chapter 1, I try to work out the details, often subtle, of Locke's man, the interrelations between man, self, person, and agent. Person is especially important, since it designates that aspect of man that carries responsibility for the actions done in this life and is the basis for judgment in the next.

The final chapter of the *Essay* offers a compendious way of organizing all of the material in that long work. Besides the familiar division of the sciences, of disciplines, or areas of knowledge into three groups, Locke has another three-fold division of what he terms provinces of 'the intellectual world'. After some discussion of Locke's attitude towards the universe itself, I explore the features of that intellectual world in chapter 2. One of the more significant features of Locke's account is an expanded notion of natural science to include speculation about bodies and spirits. Natural science may thus lead to theology.

There is another, different intellectual world that flits in and out of his discussion of the first one, the world of God, Angels and Spirits. That world has great importance for Locke and, he firmly believed, for everyone concerned about happiness and misery in the next life. It is rather surprising to discover how many references there are in the *Essay* to spirits, his frequent reference being to 'separate spirits' or 'other intelligent Beings'. Scholars and readers of Locke, myself included, have not paid much attention, if any, to this feature of the *Essay*. In my *John Locke and the Way of Ideas* (1956), I reproduced a passage from the "Epistle to the Reader" in which Locke said, "*I have been told that a short Epitome of this Treatise, which was printed in 1688, was by some condemned without reading, because in-nate* Ideas *were denied in it*" (p. 10). I apparently paid no attention to the rest of that sentence, which explains why the *Essay* was condemned: "*they too hastily concluding, that if innate* Ideas *were not supposed, there would be little left, either of the Notion or Proof of Spirits*". In that book, I focused on the innate idea controversy, ignoring entirely the reference to spirits.[1] Locke urged those who "*take the like Offence at the Entrance of this Treatise*" to read this book through. He was confident they would "*be convinced, that the taking away false foundations, is not to the prejudice, but advantage of Truth*" (p. 10). Among the false foundations was the doctrine of innate ideas and principles. The first book of the *Essay* devoted four chapters to a careful critique (demolition) of that doctrine. The innate-ideas debate was of course of great importance for its defenders, mainly divines and theologians. Locke did not give such concentrated attention to the notion of spirits as he did to that of innate ideas, but the *Essay* contains extensive references to them spread throughout that book. There is a remark in *Essay* 1.4.9, which I cite in chapter 3 below, according to which Locke may have anticipated those early objections: the lack of a notion or idea or even a name for angels or spirits is no argument against there being such Beings. Moreover, there is an extensive account later in the *Essay* on how we form ideas of spirits, as well as of God. So far from the rejection of innate ideas preventing the formation of ideas of spirits, Locke supplies details on how those ideas can be formed. Readers of the *Essay* should have been convinced that angels and spirits were not dismissed from Locke's consideration. Chapters 3, 4, and 5 attempt to bring together the various references to angels and separate spirits, and the ways in which these Beings are related to Locke's man. In this way, I hope to correct my earlier oversight of that significant remark in the "Epistle to the Reader".

Chapter 6 offers some general remarks about the relation between the two intellectual worlds and Locke's moral and affective, even aesthetic, attitudes towards the second intellectual world. That chapter also has some discussion of several comments Locke makes in his *Essays on the Law of Nature* about reason's ability to make discoveries of the obscure and hidden, and apparently even 'things' beyond meaning, albeit with the help of sense perception. The 'things' are not specified. My suggestion is that early confidence in reason is replaced by or aided by conjecture in the *Essay concerning Human Understanding*. Four different methodologies are found in Locke's writings, the method of conjecture is one that is particularly relevant to his interest in the second intellectual world. I conclude with some brief suggestions about the relation between the second intellectual world and the Kingdom of God or of the Messiah in his *Reasonableness*.

Locke's 1690 *Essay* was not given the title, 'An Essay concerning the Understanding of Man'. It was *human* understanding that he investigated. Early in the "Epistle to the Reader" he expressed the hope that, given the vanity and ignorance of much of the learned world, his treatise may be of "*some service to Humane Understanding*" (p. 10); he closes the *Essay* by classifying "all that can fall within the compass of Humane Understanding" (4.21.1). In between, there is much discussion and analysis of the understanding, with the occasional reminder that it is human understanding that is the subject of the book. Section 8 of book 1, chapter 1, refers to "the Occasion of this

Enquiry into humane Understanding"; 2.11.5 refers to "the Prerogative of Humane Understanding" in drawing certain conclusions about ideas; the chapter on the abuse of words identifies some of the "Gibberish, which in the weakness of Humane Understanding, serves so well to palliate Men's Ignorance, and cover their Errours" (3.10.14); the discussion of the extent of human knowledge cites "the Weakness of humane Understanding" (4.3.16); and the chapter on maxims speaks of "finding out intermediate *Ideas*, that shew'd the Agreement or Disagreement of the *Ideas*" as "the great Exercise and Improvement of Humane Understanding" (4.7.11).

The analysis of knowledge is as pervasive as that of the understanding. In explaining his purpose in writing the *Essay* (or in the research that went into the writing) he states explicitly that it is human knowledge that is to be examined: the "Original, Certainty, and Extent of humane Knowledge" (1.1.2). As with the understanding, he does not always modify the term 'knowledge' with 'human' but, except for some later sections which I discuss in chapter 3 where he talks of the knowledge of God, Angels and Spirits, it is clear that he is analyzing human knowledge throughout. There are a few explicit references to such knowledge. For example, the discussion of innate principles makes the point that if any idea was imprinted, it would be that of God, whose workmanship we are. Such imprinting (which Locke rejects) would mark "the first instances of humane Knowledge" (1.4.13), and 2.11.15 concludes that the previous sections of that chapter have given the "true *History of the first beginnings of Humane Knowledge*". The chapter on the abuse of words criticizes those who apply old words to "new and ambiguous Terms", thereby confounding the ordinary meanings. This is offered as an example of "the imperfection of Humane Knowledge" (3.10.6). Chapter 3 of book 4 is devoted to the extent of human knowledge, and section 6 expresses the optimistic conviction that "Humane Knowledge, under the present Circumstances of our Beings and Constitutions may be carried much farther, than it hitherto has been". In *Essay* 4.15.2 Locke concludes that he has met part of the expressed purpose of the treatise: he has "found out the bounds of humane Knowledge". The final chapter recommends "the Consideration then of *Ideas* and *Words,* as the great Instruments of Knowledge", especially for those "who would take a view of humane Knowledge in the whole Extent of it" (4.21.4).

There is a small cluster of words relating to the mind and its faculties where Locke attaches 'human' to them. In the discussion of memory he cites Pascal who, it was said, "forgot nothing of what he had done, read, or thought in any part of his rational Age" (2.10.9). Pascal's memory in this way was similar to but still inferior to the memories of "the several degrees of Angels". One difference is that "Mr. *Pascal* was still with the narrowness, that humane Minds are confin'd to here, of having great variety of *Ideas* only in succession, not [as with angels] all at once". The discussion of knowledge much later suggests that keeping a long chain of particular ideas in view, as in a complex demonstration, "may be well thought beyond the reach of humane Faculties" (4.1.9). Reason is one of the faculties of the human mind. Moral rules are characterized as "deductions of Humane Reason"; they are not innate, as some thought (1.3.12). Many also claimed the idea of God to be innate. Locke recognized that "the knowledge of a *GOD,* . . . [is] the most natural discovery of humane Reason, yet *the Idea of him, is not innate*" (1.4.17). The intellect, not often mentioned by Locke, comes in for a brief comment: "the first Capacity of Humane Intellect, is, That the mind is fitted to receive the Impressions made on it" (2.1.24).

There are also references to and some discussion of 'human life' (1.3.16; 3.10.3; 3.10.8, 12; 4.12.11), 'human species' (3.6.22, 26); "strange Issues of humane Birth" (3.3.17); "several humane *Foetus*" (3.6.26; 4.4.16); 'human shape' (1.4.16; 2.30.5; 3.6.27). 'Human nature' is another important concept, and virtue is described as the highest perfection of it (1.3.5). The "Frailties and Inconveniencies of humane Nature" come in for comment (3.9.23; 4.2.1). One of the more central references to human nature comes when Locke discusses sense certainty: "I can no more doubt, whilst I write this, that I see White and Black, and that something really exists, that causes that Sensation in me, than that I write or move my Hand; which is a Certainty as great, as humane Nature is capable of, concerning the Existence of any thing, but a Man's self alone, and of GOD" (4.11.2).[2]

There are other occurrences of 'human' modifying terms in Locke's discussion of social practice, action, and liberty. There is, for example, a curious remark about virtue and human practice in his discussion of innate practical principles. Arguing that the principle, *"That Vertue join'd with Piety, is the best Worship of God"* is not innate, he goes on to say, "the name, or sound *Vertue*, is so hard to be understood; liable to so much uncertainty in its signification; and the thing it stands for, so much contended about, and difficult to be known" (1.3.17). The uncertainty about what virtue is leads Locke to conclude that it "can be but a very uncertain Rule of Humane Practice". Given the importance of virtue for Locke, we are rather taken aback by this remark because of Locke's suggestion about its uncertainty. Of course, in this passage he is showing that this principle is not universally accepted and is given different interpretations in different societies, universality being what some appealed to as marks of innateness. Moreover, even if we recognize that "the true and only measure of Vertue" is God's Will or "the Rule prescribed by God," the dictum *'Vertue is the best Worship of God'* will be of little use in "humane Life" unless we know what God commands. So to claim as an innate principle that *"God is pleased with the doing of what he commands"* teaches very little about what he commands. Thus, that principle could hardly function as a certain innate principle (1.3.18). Later in this chapter, Locke argues that the principles employed in daily life are usually those acquired from living in a family or from education, unexamined principles that are not innate. It is not surprising that this is so, given "the Nature of Mankind, and the Constitution of Humane Affairs" (1.3.24). Most men, he says, *"cannot live, without employing their time in the daily Labours of their Callings; nor be at quiet in their Minds, without some Foundation or Principles to rest their Thoughts on"*.[3]

Uneasiness was a central concept in Locke's account of action. While discussing pleasure and pain, he remarks that uneasiness is "the chief if not only spur to humane Industry and

Action" (2.20.6). The final chapter defines ethics as "the seeking out those Rules, and Measures of humane Action, which lead to Happiness, and the Means to practice them" (4.21.3). Moral relations are characterized as "the Relations of humane Actions to a Law" (2.28.17). An earlier section in this chapter on moral relations identifies human action as a mixed mode (2.28.4). Further comments on human action as mixed modes can be found in 3.5.7.

Many other aspects of what it is to be human are spread throughout the *Essay*. A quick list will serve to fill out those I have mentioned so far. Such a list also gives added evidence of the wide scope of the topics to be found in the *Essay*.

Human soul—2.1.18
Human liberty—2.21.56, 71
Human laws—2.27.20, 22; 3.9.9
Human identity—2.27.21
Human capacity—3.3.2; 4.12.7
Human science—4.3.10
Human testimony—4.16.5
Human senses and observation—4.16.12
Human sagacity—4.17.11
Human certainty—4.17.14

In calling attention to the frequent use of 'human', or 'humane', in the *Essay*, I have two reasons: first as a reminder that while 'man' usually appears in Locke's narrative, that term is really a proxy for 'human'. It is the nature of what it is to be human that is Locke's concern, at least so much of human nature as our limited knowledge reveals. The second and more important reason is that it marks off the sphere of the human from the non-human, or rather, the 'more than human', the other intelligent Beings in the universe about which Locke comments in various passages. That part of the *Essay*, that portion of Locke's thought, has not been given much serious attention, so it seems to me worth our time to explore what he has to say not so much about God but about angels and what he refers to as 'other spirits'. Since the human soul turns out to be one of those spirits among the ranks of spirits, we can locate man, human finite Beings, on the chain of being. We can in this way trace some of the theological implications of the doctrines of the *Essay*.

The *Essay* is a complex, comprehensive work. Just viewing its overall structure of four books, the subject-matter is knowledge, language, and ideas. Within each of these books, a host of now standard issues, topics, problems, and theories can be found relating to human experience from infancy to adulthood on such topics as the need for clarity of expression and understanding, the role of science in human affairs, the nature and function of mental faculties and powers, the importance of virtue and moral action, the existence of God, the role of faith and reason, and much more. The chapter on identity and diversity, chapter 27 of the second book, concerns human identity, the identity of man and the moral person. That chapter is (as Etienne Balibar characterizes it in his excellent book[4]) a treatise in itself, an essay within the *Essay*. It is, in many ways, a key chapter with its distinctions between physical and moral man, the stress upon the moral aspect of the agent of action. That chapter is pivotal, casting man in the dual role of cognizer and moral actor, the latter being concerned for happiness in this and the next world.

Because the *Essay* is such a complex, topic-laden work with comments and analyses often scattered through chapters and sections, it is sometimes useful, even necessary, to track the occurrences of particular words and phrases, specific concepts and doctrines. An inventory of word usage is often helpful in our effort to discover what an author meant and believed. Such an inventory is especially appropriate for Locke. Sometimes his usage seems imprecise, or it moves between several words for what may be the same thought, such as soul, mind, and spirit; or man, self, and person; or Beings, creatures, and spirits. It is also useful to bring together and present the reader with his various remarks on a specific topic, such as the process of conceiving and what is conceivable, or the notion of the universe, or the underlying structure of matter and man.

CHAPTER ONE

LOCKE'S MAN

Much attention has been paid to Locke's discussion of personal identity, his concept of person, the distinction between man and person. In fact, in that discussion there are four terms or concepts: man, self, person, and agent. Around those terms, a number of themes, aspects of Locke's thought, are clustered, some more directly related to those terms, others more tangential but still important for our understanding of Locke's thought. If possible, some sorting of those four terms could be helpful in reaching an appreciation of the nature and function of man in his account. If we can determine who the agent of action is, find the locus of agency in acting, the source of the power, that nature may be explicated. There are similarities between the body-mind relation and the man-person relation, similarities that may again raise the question of materialism. I think we can say that Locke's man is not born a person, but that the man can become a person, can develop into one. The boy, the child, grows into a man through education, acquiring the necessary attributes of virtue and rationality. There is a rough analog between the education of a child and the emergence of personhood from a man. In Locke's discussion of man there is also a firm suggestion of an underlying constitution from which the properties come as their causal source: an intriguing parallel between the constitution of man and the corpuscular structure of body.

In this chapter, I explore these various topics, trusting that the nature of man—of a human being in Locke's account—may become a little bit more clear. Person has perhaps received too much attention; it is man's turn now.

1. Body-Mind, Man-Person

Distinctions such as Locke draws between person and man, or Kant's distinction between empirical and intelligible realms (with its apparent reference to two selves), raise a crucial question: are we to understand these distinctions as ontological or as functional differences? A distinction between soul and body, drawn by other writers in an earlier tradition, located soul and body in different ontological or metaphysical categories. Sometimes the mind-body distinction was similarly intended to mark out diverse domains. These two contrasts—soul-body and mind-body—embraced both ontological and functional categories. Mind and soul perform functions different from those of bodily processes. This ontology introduces a gap between the two functionalities of mind and body. That gap was not only explanatory, it was more decisively ontological.

If the ontological difference is retained, for example, between mind and body or between consciousness and brain processes, can the explanatory gap be closed? The answer to that question may depend upon our understanding of or our demands for explanation. If the demand is to give some account of how mental events can belong to a physical body—the question has haunted philosophers from at least Descartes to the present—the task of explaining may be difficult if not elusive, especially if what is required is some process, some activity that begins as a brain event and ends as a conscious state. Various strategies have been tried, from bold efforts to deny the apparent differences between being aware of trees and towers and the neural processes underlying those conscious experiences, to less extreme measures. Perceiving, being aware of colors and shapes, the bold effort proclaims, is just a matter of certain brain states and processes. The less extreme measures to close the gap try to have both identity and difference: mental events can be explained in terms of physical (neural) events. The explanations offered sometimes use causal language, but the causality of conscious perception by neural processes is murky at best and usually obscure. The suggestion seems to be that identifying the neural events correlated with perceptual states enables us to concentrate on the neural events, almost as if the perceptual experience does not exist. There appears to be an attempt here to say conscious states are identical to brain states, even while talking of correlations between brain and mind, between neural events and consciousness. Sometimes it is said that mental states are realized in physical states. 'Correlated with', 'realized in', or 'caused by' cannot escape the differences, certainly not the functional differences. It may even be difficult to escape from an ontological difference as well.

Are there parallel problems in understanding or interpreting Locke's contrast between person and man, or Kant's empirical and intelligible selves?[1] When Locke conjectures that thought could be a property of some organized bit of matter (e.g., the brain), some readers in Locke's day and in our own saw that suggestion as a form of materialism. Among writers today, Nicholas Jolley is one who reads Locke that way. Jolley links the thinking-matter suggestion, "consciousness may inhere in a material system",[2] with Locke's account of personal identity. That linkage is made by Locke's remarks that immortality does not require an immaterial substance. Jolley asserts that Locke offers "a theory of personal identity which points the moral that the survival of the person beyond death does not depend logically on the truth of substantial dualism".[3] Jolley talks as if this rejection of the necessity of an immaterial substance for immortality is "Locke's whole theory of personal identity", that theory "is carefully crafted to be consistent with the doctrine of materialism".[4]

Of course, Locke's theory or account of personal identity involves much more than the theological issue of immortality and the question of immaterial substance. Nor does Locke link his suggestion of thinking matter with what he says about personal identity and the distinction between person and man. The status of thought or consciousness is important for personal identity, so we do need to ask 'what would happen to consciousness were it to be a property of the brain?' Would the result be a materialism, as Jolley and others seem to think? If so, thought or consciousness would have to be a physical property, and we would have property-reduction, not property dualism. But from what Locke says about his suggestion, and from the explication he gave to Bishop Stillingfleet, it does not sound as if he understands his suggestion as eliminating thought as a mental property, as a property different in kind from extension. There is also an interesting remark in *An Essay concerning Human Understanding* 2.1.15 in which Locke is arguing against the Cartesian thesis that the soul always thinks. Locke suggests an argument that might be used to support the Cartesian thesis. "Perhaps it will be said, that in a waking Man, the materials of the Body are employ'd, and made use of, in thinking; and that the memory of Thoughts, is retained by the impressions that are made on the Brain, and the traces there left after such thinking. . . ." The argument goes on to suggest that when a man sleeps and does not dream, and hence seems not to think, that is because in sleep the soul thinks apart from the body and hence leaves no brain traces. It is not clear whether the suggestion in the first part of this passage is that thinking in the waking man is the brain impressions, or just that in that kind of thinking there are brain correlates. But since Locke does refer to animal spirits elsewhere and even uses a neurophysiological argument to explain the hot and cold feelings in hands immersed in water, I think we can say Locke was open to filling in the explanatory gap with such accounts, even as the causal explanation of perception.[5] He would not have intended such neurophysiological explanations to reduce thought to brain impressions. The thinking-matter suggestion offers us a property dualism: the brain, under this hypothesis, would have two kinds of properties. Property dualism would replace substance dualism. We may find it difficult, as did many of Locke's contemporaries, to understand how a mental property could belong to a physical mechanism. For Locke such a feat was possible for God, so perhaps it should not be surprising if we have difficulty understanding or making sense of the result. But to conclude that Locke's suggestion, coupled with his claim that immortality does not require an immaterial substance, results in a materialism, even if Locke did not intend such a result, is to overlook the nature of property dualism.

Moreover, we need to ask 'what would be the implication for Locke's full account of personal identity?' were materialism the product of those two doctrines. Jolley says only that the theory of personal identity is consistent with materialism, but what would a materialist account of personal identity be? Are the other components of Locke's account of personal identity (the consciousness of my actions, the acceptance of responsibility for them, the person as a moral agent) really consistent with materialism? If the person is identified with the man, does that not yield some kind of materialism or corporealism? The answer to this question depends upon what 'man' stands for. If man is just the functioning body, and if person is the same as man, this would be some kind of corporealism. Locke does say that the ordinary way of speaking makes the person and the man one: "the same Person, and the same Man, stand for one and the same thing...".[6] Section 20 of that same chapter on identity and diversity says that the word 'I' can stand for either the man or the person, depending upon the circumstances. In the example he considered, of the loss of memory of an action, the 'I' applied to the man only, but "the same Man being presumed to be the same Person", the first person pronoun refers to both man and person.

Man is a biological organism; 'same man' designates "a participation of the same continued Life, by constantly fleeting Particles of Matter [biological matter], in succession vitally united to the same organized Body".[7] We might say man consists of two materialities, corporeal particles and a biological body. But Locke says elsewhere that by the term 'man' we mean "a corporeal rational Creature".[8] The term 'rational' clearly adds a non-corporeal property to the corporeal, biological body. Since Locke characterized 'person' as having reason, 'rational' added to 'man' indicates that man and person are not separated or distinct, same reference for 'I' but different contributions to the combination of man and person. Person adds something important to man, rationality is added to corporeality. So we can say, I think, that Locke's account of personal identity is not consistent with materialism, the properties of a person—intelligence, rationality, consciousness—are not identified with or reduced to neurobiological properties nor to material particles.

2. Action and Agency

The question now is, how do man and person work together, how does agency pertain to the man-person, what is the locus of agency? To say, 'I did it', e.g. repayment of a debt, is to say I performed that action in a certain way, with arm or hands or by instructing my banker, etc. Actions require a body, a physical body. As actor, I am both a person and a man. Thus, I am the agent of my actions. We need to ask 'does the agency pertain to the unit of man and person?' or 'are there aspects of agency ascribed to the man, others ascribed to the person?' On Locke's account, agency involves power. If we consult the main chapter of the *Essay* where Locke discusses agency and action, 2.21, we find that the majority of actions locates the power of acting and deciding with the man. One section at least locates that power with the person: liberty belongs "to the Person having the Power of doing, or forbearing to do".[9] Several sections give the mind some power relevant to acting. Other passages just refer to 'the agent'. Frequent references to man and agent occur in the same passage.

Essay 2.21.8 credits the man with the power to think and to move, thinking and moving being the two categories of action. A man is free when he can move according to the preference of his mind. Section 15 characterizes liberty as "the power a Man has to do or forbear doing any particular Action" (see also §§47, 52). The next section (§16) speaks of freedom, suggesting that it can be "attributed to the Power, that is in a Man, to produce, or forbear producing Motion in parts of his Body, by choice or preference". Section 18 refers to "different Powers in the Mind, or in the Man, to do several Actions"; and section 19 asserts again that "it is the Man that does the Action". The discussion of freedom and liberty cites several specific actions preformed by a man, e.g., walking, standing still, falling from a precipice (§24), falling into the water (§9). Later sections ascribe to a man uneasiness, the spur to act. Many sections refer to man as free or constrained (e.g., §§8, 9, 11, 12, 21–25, 28, 30, 34).

Some passages mix man and person, as in 2.21.10: "Again, suppose a Man be carried, whilst fast asleep, into a Room, where is a Person he longs to see and speak with". Is a sleeping man not a person? In 2.27.15, Locke speaks of the person at the resurrection but goes on to ask whether it would be the same man. Section 22 of this same chapter opens with the question: "But is not a Man Drunk and Sober the same Person?" Many passages just refer to the agent of action: the "Power in any Agent to do or forbear any particular Action" (2.21.8), "an Agent capable of Volition" (2.21.13), "whatever Agent has a power to think on its own Actions" (2.21.15), "it is the Agent that has power, or is able to" act (2.21.19). As I noted above, this last passage has the man doing the action, but the power belongs to the agent. Is the agent then different from the man? That section actually offers a three-fold distribution: "But it is the Mind that operates, and exerts these Powers [of choosing and thinking]; it is the Man that does the Action [of singing and dancing], it is the Agent that has power, or is able to do" (2.21.19).[10] 'Operating', 'exerting' and 'doing' are all power terms, designating active contributions to the result. In other words, (1) the power of the mind forms preferences, makes a choice, (2) the man dances and sings because (3) the man as agent possesses the power of acting. Three different powers: of the mind, of the man, and of the agent. Agency-power may be the same as man-power.[11] If we can think of an inactive man, a man for the moment not doing anything, such a man at that moment would not be an agent, although, if he was forbearing to do, I guess he would be an agent. Locke's example of a man asleep while carried into another room would be an example of a man who, at that time, would not be an agent. The change in a man from passive to active marks a change from being a man to being an agent (and perhaps a person). Agency depends upon the man—he is an agent because he is a man.

The headings in the table of contents for sections 14–21 read, "Liberty belongs not to the Will . . . But to the Agent or Man". The 'or' in this last phrase may be ambiguous, meaning the agent is the man, or that the two differ. Earlier chapters refer to the free agent (1.3.14) and to sensible or voluntary agents (2.20.14). Later sections in 2.21 have the agent exercising the power that it or he has (§§29, 72; see 2.27.29). The agent is free (§50) and has the liberty to act in consequence of thoughts (§71). Section 13 of 2.27 even has "consciousness of past Actions" annexed to an individual agent, and 4.21.1 ascribes rationality and volition to agents, in his quick description of ethics: "that which a Man himself ought to do, as a rational and voluntary Agent".[12]

What this brief examination of passages about agency reveals is how important was Locke's notion of power. Both the physical and social domains are pervaded by powers, active powers.[13] God too is an agent—a wise and understanding agent with powers (4.3.28, 4.20.15). Where there is agency, there is power, the power to produce physical changes in objects and in sense organs, the power to move one's own limbs, to act in accordance with one's preferences. The power or ability to act morally—to repay debts, to tell the truth, to help others—involves the mind as well as the body. Such actions involve intentions, knowledge, a sense of responsibility, respect for others. The knowledge relevant to moral actions is the knowledge of the laws of nature, the moral laws on which society is founded and which are to govern our actions.

We can also say that these passages confirm that it is one 'entity' that has the power, decides and acts. Whether we speak of the man, the person or the agent, the reference is the same. We cannot say the referent is a substance, although perhaps the physical body might count as a material substance, even though on Locke's account we have no knowledge of body as the traditional substance. Certainly it is clear that 'person' does not refer to a substance, material or immaterial. E. J. Lowe has recently suggested that we take the referent to be a psychological substance, meaning, I guess, that we are dealing with properties (e.g., rationality, intention, consciousness) that belong to something, to a conscious being.[14] But if the core, as it were, of the man-person, of the unit that is man, person, and agent, is the human body with its biology and neurophysiology, then mind and consciousness become properties of that body. It is precisely in this way that Jolley's claim that Locke's account of the person is consistent with materialism has some root, except that those properties of the body (of the brain) do not, on Locke's account, become physical (neural) properties. Man, a human, starts out as an embryo, becomes an infant, an adult, and an old man. Man also becomes a person, when certain conditions are met.

The term 'person' frequently has a moral tone in Locke's account of personal identity, but it may be too strong to say that that is its only feature. It might even be possible to distinguish 'self' from 'person', the latter carrying the moral connotation, the former referring to self-identity. The agent of action is the man, the self. Actions are not restricted to moral actions: dancing or singing, fencing or talking are actions of the agent as much as are truth-telling, helping others, honoring parents. It is these latter, moral actions, that enable Locke to give his most striking (chilling) example of a person becoming a man, or sinking even lower: those agents in Locke's *Two Treatises of Government* who violate the law of nature, thereby becoming like (and can be treated as) wild savage beasts. The locus of action in their case was the self, but they did not behave as persons.

3. Secular Self, Moral Self

Is there some textual basis for a distinction between self and person? Or is *'self'* just another term, along with 'man', 'person', and 'agent' for specifying and referring to the subject who thinks and acts? There is a difference of tone at least between speaking of 'my self' and 'my person'. We may be self-confident, but hardly person-confident. We can be self-ish but not person-ish. To say I am concerned for my person sounds rather formal. It would be more natural to be concerned for my self, even for my body (my arms, legs, fingers). We might ask 'who was the person at the door?', although it is more natural to simply ask 'who was at the door ?' We would not ask 'Who was the self at the door?'

Are these linguistic conventions reflected in Locke's use of *'self'* and *'person'*? Of these two terms, *'self'* seems to be the more basic. If we survey the sections in 2.27, we find (a) a number of sections in which consciousness determines the self; (b) that there are also two sections that mix self and person in the discussion; and (c) that there are several sections that apply to the self the talk of being concerned. It is tempting to suggest that the (a) sections present what we might call the 'secular self', in opposition to person as the 'moral self'.

3.1. On Being Self to Self

The first section in which this curious phrase appears is in 2.27.9, the definition of 'person' as a "thinking intelligent Being, that has reason and reflection, and can consider it self as it self".[15] Consciousness is the means for such consideration. Specifically, in sensing and perceiving, "every one is to himself, that which he calls *self*". The identity of the person rests on the sameness of self: "And as far as this consciousness can be extended backwards to any past Action or Thought, so far reaches the identity of that *Person*; it is the same *self* now as it was then; and 'tis by the same *self* with this present one that now reflects on it, that that Action was done". Locke employs the term 'Being' as a way to avoid 'substance'. He also uses the phrase 'thinking thing' in a similar way. That thinking thing is, he seems to say, a self; over time, via consciousness, it is "the same to it self". When consciousness is interrupted by forgetfulness, we lose "sight of our past *selves*" (§10). The curious phrase 'personal self' occurs in section 10. Same consciousness over time reveals the same personal self. The link between consciousness and self is explicitly stated in the table of contents for 2.27.17, "Self depends on Consciousness", and in section 23, "Consciousness alone makes self".[16]

Section 10 ended with his remark that the same consciousness unites "those distant Actions into the same Person, whatever Substances contributed to their Production". It is not same substance that accounts for the person, but the sameness of consciousness. Section 11 then offers evidence for that remark. "That this is so, we have some kind of Evidence in our very Bodies, all whose Particles, whilst vitally united to this same thinking conscious self, so that we feel when they are touch'd, and are affected by, and conscious of good or harm that happens to them, are a part of our *selves: i.e.* of our thinking conscious *self*". The referent of 'this' in the first clause of this sentence is not entirely clear. If the reference is to the first clause of the final sentence of section 10, the consciousness that unites actions and constitutes the person is said to depend upon the body. That dependence would seem to show that it is not consciousness alone that makes the person; at least not consciousness acting apart from the body. What is touched and affected are, I think, the particles, or more precisely, the parts of our body. If the 'this' at the beginning of this sentence refers to the last clause of section 10, "whatever Substances contributed to their Production", is the body offered as a 'substance' which contributes to the production of action?[17] We seem to have here another indication of Locke's recognition of the role of the body (of nerves and brain) in sensing and perceiving. Section 25 confirms the relation between self and body: "Thus any part of our Bodies vitally united to that, which is conscious in us, makes a part of our *selves*". Corporeal particles are 'vitally united' to the thinking conscious self. The nature of that vital union is left obscure. I take Locke simply to be saying that because there is a vital link between those particles and our being aware of being touched and affected (after our body parts have been affected), we recognize that the body is our body, part of our self. The phrase, 'conscious self' goes along with 'personal self', giving again priority to the self.

Section 13 raises the question of why "one intellectual [i.e., immaterial] Substance may not have represented to it, as done by it self" some actions that it never did. Section 14 says again that if our consciousness fails to include some past action, an action in fact done by others, we would not be one self with those others. Section 21 repeats the point that it is consciousness "alone which makes what we call *self*". Section 23 insists that "*self* is not determined by Identity or Diversity of Substance", only by identity of consciousness. Section 24 speaks of a 'Man's self', a phrase that also occurs in section 25.[18]

3.2. Person and Self

We saw above that 2.27.9 includes in its account of what 'person' stands for the fact that the thinking being can "consider it self as it self". Section 17 contains that curious example of a finger being cut off: should consciousness "go along with the little Finger, and leave the rest of the Body, 'tis evident the little Finger would be the *Person*".[19] Under that condition, the self then "would have nothing to do with the rest of the Body". Self and person go together. Section 26 then announces that "*Person*, as I take it, is the name for this *self*". The next sentence reserves the term 'person' for the use of others, a kind of third-person use: "Where-ever a Man finds, what he calls *himself*, there I think another may say is the same *Person*". I am not sure what to make of 'person' being the name for '*self*'. We have to be careful not to make too much of this passing remark. 'Man' is also said to be a name in several other passages (2.28.15; 2.32.25); 2.27.7 raises the possibility that person, man, and substance are "three Names standing for three different Ideas".[20] Nevertheless, the term person as the name of the self does raise several questions. Is there a suggestion that 'person' is only a name, that it does not mark or stand for a sort or kind, that it is not an ontological category? In distinguishing person from man, is more implied than that 'person' is merely a name? If person is more than a name, what can we say about persons?

While discussing true and false ideas, Locke remarks that when we ask "what it is" of some "new Thing of a kind" that we do not recognize, we mean by that question "nothing but the Name" (2.32.7).[21] If I ask, "What is it that is self to it self?" the answer in terms of this passage would be "person," a name. But that name would apply, I take it, to anyone who is conscious of self, who is self to self. Does that general application indicate that 'person' designates a class or kind? If the suggestions of Lowe and Parmentier are taken seriously—that person (for Lowe) is a psychological substance or (for Parmentier) person is a new category replacing, as I would say, the traditional substance doctrine—then person may be more basic than self. The problem for both Descartes and Locke was how to characterize the union of mind and body in man. Such a union fell outside the usual two-substance doctrine. The notion of an incomplete substance may have been Descartes's attempt to find a different category for man. Similarly, but perhaps for different reasons (our lack of any knowledge about substance), Locke may have employed the term 'person' as a substitute category.

It has been the term 'person' that framed the debates around Locke's discussion from his day to the present. In that way, 'person' is the more familiar term, not self. The two terms have almost equal occurrences in 2.27. It may not be too important to decide which term is more basic, especially if Locke ascribes most of the same properties or features to both. There are several definitions that may help us decide whether there is a distinction between self and person.

> Definition 1: "This being premised to find wherein *personal Identity* consists, we must consider what *Person* stands for; which, I think, is a thinking intelligent Being, that has reason and reflection, and can consider it self as it self, the same thinking thing in different times and places;

which it does only by that consciousness, which is inseparable from thinking, and as it seems to me essential to it . . ." (2.27.9).

No moral overtones here, just the specification of intelligence, reason, reflection and the considering of self by self. The formation of, or the realization by the self of its self, is what a person is on this definition. The second definition of person is the more familiar:

> Definition 2: It is a "Forensick Term appropriating Actions and their Merit; and so belongs only to intelligent Agents capable of a Law, and Happiness and Misery. This personality extends it *self* beyond present Existence to what is past, only by consciousness, whereby it becomes concerned and accountable, owns and imputes to it *self* past Actions . . ." (2.27.26).

The difference between these two definitions might be characterized as the difference between a cognitive consciousness and an affective or even a moral consciousness.[22] What is curious about this second definition is, as I remarked earlier, the third-person sound to the ascription of 'person' to a self: others may say it is the same self, so long as the intelligent being finds what he calls himself. That remark follows the opening sentence about 'person' being the name of self. It would be tempting to say the term 'person' has both a first-person reference in 2.27.9 and a third-person reference in 2.27.26. But the intelligent being considers himself to be a self, not a person. Consciousness constitutes a self, but in so doing, a person is also formed. The second definition refers to the ascription (by others only?) of responsibility for the actions of that self. So we can say that 'person' names the self of both definitions. That name embraces both a secular and a moral self. The new category suggested by Parmentier thus plays a substantive or, better, a subject role. In that way, 'person' would be the more fundamental term.

3.3. Self-Concern

The link between self in the second definition and person becomes more explicit in other sections where the language of 'concern' is applied to the self. The term 'concern' plays a central role in the account of person as a moral agent.[23] So self and person become closely connected, perhaps even interchangeable. Writing in the first person, Locke says that, "had I the same consciousness, that I saw the Ark and *Noah*'s Flood, as that I saw an overflowing of the *Thames* last Winter, or as that I write now, I could no more doubt that I, that write this now, that saw the *Thames* overflow'd last Winter, and that view'd the Flood at the general Deluge, was the same *self*, place that *self* in what Substance you please, than that I that write this am the same *my self* now whilst I write" (2.27.16). He goes on to stress the fact that "as to this point of being the same *self*, it matters not whether this present *self* be made up of the same or other Substances, I being as much concern'd, and as justly accountable for any Action was done a thousand Years since, appropriated to me now by this self-consciousness, as I am, for what I did the last moment".[24] Section 17 is even more forthright in employing the affective language for the self. It captures all of the properties that characterize the person: consciousness "makes the same *Person*", thereby constituting what he calls the "inseparable *self*"; the person attributes its actions to "it *self*, and owns all the Actions". Section 25 reiterates the concern for self: "This every intelligent Being, sensible of Happiness or Misery, must grant, that there is something that is *himself*, that he is concerned for, and would have happy . . .". Section 26 picks up this association of happiness and misery with the self and applies it to the person.[25]

4. Physical Man, Rational Man, Moral Man

My suggested thesis that the term *'self'* designates a 'secular self', as opposed to or distinguished from 'person' as a moral self, does not have any systematic support from Locke's usage in these passages, but the two definitions of 'person' do establish a dual function for consciousness: a cognitive and a moral or affective constituting of self and person. The cognitive constituting is a necessary condition for the moral or affective self or person. We may have a choice between (a) speaking of two aspects of self, or (b) treating these aspects as self and person. In the first choice, personal identity spans both aspects, so we could distinguish a secular from a moral self. In the alternative, the term 'person' identifies the moral, affective aspect. On this alternative, we can cite two features of the self that are different from person. (1) The self and the body, even body parts, have a clear attachment.[26] (2) The self also seems to be more basic than person in a temporal sense, the person grows out of the self, the self can be called a person (its name is 'person') when certain conditions are met in character-formation.[27] When a self earns the name of 'person', that is a mark of its moral maturity. When we ask how we should understand Locke's distinction between man and person, I suggest we can say 'person' adds, or at least stresses, the forensic, law-abiding features to the self, creating what Locke calls 'moral man', a self concerned for happiness and virtue in this life and ultimately salvation in the next (3.11.16).[28]

Locke's discussion of action and the various powers involved indicates that some actions are moral actions, others various physical actions. What makes any action my action, is the consciousness I have of doing them. In this way, whether it be an act of singing or dancing, of walking by the Thames when it was frozen, of experimenting with different hands in water, chopping an almond, or whether it is actions such as repaying a debt, honoring parents, helping others, consciousness forms a self or a person. My attempt to say the first group of actions belongs to the self, while the second belongs to the person, does not quite fit the texts, although there are only a few passages that speak of the self in those forensic tones usually reserved for person. Keeping in mind the 3.11.16 passage just cited, we may have some basis for speaking of a continuum from man in a physical sense, to man as rational (perhaps the self), to moral man (the person). Each item along this line possesses powers, physical powers, powers of thinking and acting, and moral powers. The mature individual, the unit of man, self, and person, is the locus of all these powers. Agency is located in this unit, the man as agent of thought and action is both self and person.

5. Definitions of Man

In locating the source of agency in the unit of man, self and person, Locke takes account of the role of man (especially physical man) and person in action. Bodily motion and conscious intentions are joint components in all human action. His reference to the particles of matter and body-parts being vitally united with, even being parts of the conscious self, is an emphatic recognition of the dual involvement of body and mind in action. Locke does not give us any details on how the physiology of the body, the system of animal spirits, is tied to the self, but he makes use of physiology in explaining some sensory experiences. Most often he confesses ignorance of the way in which sensation is caused by physical events outside and inside the body. But he assigns that vital union which particles of matter have with the self also to the body: "the Identity of the same *Man* consists . . . in nothing but a participation of the same continued Life, by constantly fleeting Particles of Matter, in succession vitally united to the same organized Body" (2.27.6; cf. 2.27.8). The vital union of material particles with the body is presumably of a different sort from the vital union of those particles with the conscious self. 'Union' and 'part of' are left unanalyzed.

In the 2.27.8 passage, Locke identifies the 2.27.6 remark as a definition, adding that "the *Idea* in our Minds, of which the Sound *Man* in our Mouths is the Sign, is nothing but of an Animal of such a certain Form [i.e., shape]" (2.27.8). When he says that "ingenuous observation puts it past doubt" that the word 'man' is a sign of animal with a specific shape, he seems to be reporting on common usage among his contemporaries.[29] For Locke, definition is not a matter of giving the genus and differentia. Rather, it is the enumeration of the simple ideas comprising some complex idea (3.3.10). This is the best way to make "another understand by Words, what *Idea* the term defined stands for". In the example from 2.27.8, the idea of man contains the ideas of animal and of a specific shape. He cites other definitions in 3.3.10, but there is no indication whether he accepts either of them. Notice the way he starts the first definition:

> Definition 1: "if it should be said, that Man was a solid extended Substance, having Life, Sense, spontaneous Motion, and the Faculty of Reasoning", the meaning of that word would be understood.

> Definition 2: Man is "a *rational Animal;* which by the several definitions of *Animal, Vivens,* and *Corpus,* resolves it self into those enumerated *Ideas*".

The first definition also occurs in 3.6.3 with some variation: "[perhaps], voluntary Motion, with Sense and Reason, join'd to a Body of a certain shape, be the complex *Idea,* to which I, and others, annex the name *Man*". The 'perhaps' leaves it open as to Locke's acceptance of this definition. In that passage, he is concerned to deny that that definition would be, or would give us, the real essence of man. It would only be the nominal essence.[30] The same point about essence is made in 3.11.16 where he cites another definition of man, one related to morality. "When we say that *Man is subject to Law:* We mean nothing by *Man,* but a corporeal rational Creature". With this definition in the context of moral discourse, shape is irrelevant: "For were there a Monkey, or any other Creature to be found, that had the use of Reason, to such a degree, as to be able to understand general Signs, and to deduce Consequences about general *Ideas,* he would no doubt be subject to Law".[31] Section 20 of this same chapter says that if shape is taken as the mark for "Creatures we count of our kind", then the definition of man (of the same man) as an idea "made up of Animality and Rationality, united in the same Subject" would not serve as well as does the definition in terms of shape for the class or kind 'man'. So perhaps different definitions are required for different purposes and functions.[32] So too for self and person.

6. The Fundamental Constitution of Man

Kinds, sorts, or classes, as far as our knowledge extends, refer only to our general abstract ideas. 'Essential' only relates to the ideas we form. When Locke says in 3.6.4, "'Tis necessary for me to be as I am; GOD and Nature has made me so", he goes on to say, "there is nothing I have, is essential to me". This latter clause can be interpreted in two ways: (a) essential relates only to classes, not to individuals, or (b) none of my properties reveal the real essence of man. Since the example here is of a particular individual, the first interpretation applies. The properties of any individual man could reveal some of the properties of the class of men, but as the (b) interpretation reminds us, Locke did not believe our knowledge reaches to real essences. The real essence of bodies or of man, if there are such essences, do not (or we cannot say they do) show up in our observations. Whether Locke thought there were real kinds in nature may be unclear from his extended discussion of essence, but it does seem that he entertained the possibility of there being an internal structure of physical bodies from which we could have a deductive science of nature.[33] Perhaps the corpuscular structure of matter may have been what he had in mind. His extended exposition of this notion of an a priori deductive science of nature serves to contrast it with experimental and observational science, the only science open to man's faculties and knowledge. The important question is whether Locke believed there were real essences in nature and real necessary connections. He certainly rejected the traditional notion of real essence, but a case can be made for saying he accepted the corpuscular theory as a replacement for the traditional theory. He did characterize the corpuscular theory as the most probable, so he left the way open for some other candidate to fill the role of the source for the observed properties of body.[34] But his acceptance of a foundational structure of matter, which is responsible for properties we discover by experience and observation, seems clear, even though such a structure was beyond our experience.

What is fascinating about his discussion of man is his rather clear albeit brief statement of such a structure for man, not just for man's body. Real essence in man, he says, would be the "Source of all those Operations, which are to be found in any Individual of that Sort. The foundation of all those Qualities, which are the Ingredients of our complex *Idea*" (3.6.3). Presumably, 'source' means 'cause'. What are the operations that are caused by the source is not clear. The operations he refers to may be some of the powers mentioned in the next passage. The 'qualities', I assume, are those referred to in the definitions of man: solid substance, life, sensation, reasoning. The source or foundation would be quite different from the qualities and operations we experience and observe. Locke then turns to the knowledge we would have, were real essence (the source) available to us. Our knowledge of man would be of the kind that Angels or God have:[35] "And had we such a Knowledge of that Constitution of *Man*, from which the Faculties of Moving, Sensation, and Reasoning, and other Powers flow; and on which his so regular shape depends . . . we should have a quite other *Idea* of his *Essence*, than what now is contained in our Definition of that *Species*, be it what it will" (3.6.3). Real essence would replace nominal essence, certain knowledge would replace experience and observation. From this remark we learn that the source also causes the faculties and powers we have, faculties of moving, sensing, and reasoning. Such knowledge would change our idea of man, even the idea of a particular, individual man "would be as far different from what it now is, as is his, who knows all the Springs and Wheels, and other contrivances within, of the famous Clock at *Strasburg*, from that which a gazing Country-man has of it, who barely sees the motion of the Hand, and hears the Clock strike, and observes only some of the outward appearances" (cf. *Essay* 3.6.9). We only have the appearances to work with, our idea of man, of a human being, is only based on our experience or on our accepted definitions.[36]

These passages seem to be in Locke's own voice. We cannot say with certainty what he may have imagined the constitution of man to be, but it would be difficult for it not to be physical or biological, perhaps both.[37] Locke seems to have taken the notion of properties 'flowing from' a hidden, theoretic source as 'deducible from' such a source; at least, he stressed this feature in order to highlight his insistence on an experimental science. But 'flow from' also marks a causal relation. If we keep in mind his clear ascription of a 'vital union' of particles of matter with both body and self, he may have had in mind the corpuscular structure of matter as the constitution for body and man, even for moral man. He does not identify the corpuscular structure as the source of intelligence or reason, but that theory does assign a causal role to corpuscles for sensation and the origin of ideas, perhaps also for the shape of physical objects. He does not mention any other fundamental structure for the properties of man. Thus, the constitution of man, self, and person may be the same as the constitution of man's body. Then the problem is to explain the causal 'flowing from' relation for the psychological or mental properties of moral man, self or person. Locke does not offer any explanation or illustration.[38]

6.1. The Constitution of Children

The 'flow from' metaphor also occurs in a different context when Locke discusses the importance of forming a good character in children. There, he refers to "Actions, which naturally flow from a well-formed Mind".[39] That same treatise contains many references to the constitution of children, of their bodies and their minds.[40] This use of 'constitution' is clearly different from that term used in the *Essay* about a deductive science of nature. There is an interesting problem, perhaps a tension, between these two uses of the notion of a constitution from which specific properties flow. If we identify the references to an underlying constitution in the *Essay* as the real essence constitution and the *Education* constitution as the constitution of character, one difference is that the latter can be formed and influenced by the guidance of parents and tutor. The role of education is in large part to build a good character, to provide for such qualities as civility, modesty, and other virtues. In helping the child form a good character, the tutor has to recognize that the child has some 'native Propensities', some 'tempers or traits' such as "Fierce or Mild, Bold or Bashful, Compassionate or Cruel, Open or Reserv'd".[41] Whether these native propensities are caused by some feature of the real essence constitution, on the basis of what Locke writes in the Education we cannot say. A few native propensities are cited in the *Essay*, "Principles of Action . . . lodged in Men's Appetites" (1.3.13), "tendencies imprinted on the Minds of Men", tendencies which "from the very first instances of Sense and Perception . . . are grateful, and others unwelcome to them; some things that they incline to, and others that they fly" (1.3.3). He does not suggest that these tendencies or traits 'flow from the underlying constitution of man. There is not, of course, a detailed or clearly developed theory of what features of man do flow from, are caused by the real essence constitution. Nevertheless, we can fill in some details of a general concept of man, of a human being.

We know from the early books of the *Essay* that the physical organism, even prenatally, experiences some sensations of warmth and light; after birth, specific ideas are gradually acquired. There are no native or innate truths but, as we just saw, there is a practical innate principle or tendency to seek pleasure and avoid pain. We can also say that, despite Locke's use of the white sheet or blank tablet metaphor, the organism has a number of faculties, at least the necessary equipment for the functions of sensation, memory, and reason. From the *Education* we learn that the child is born with certain traits which parents and the tutor must acknowledge and work with in leading the child to become a rational, moral person. Then from the brief passage in *Essay* 3.6.3, we know that Locke at least entertained the notion of an underlying structure (probably corpuscular) which causes some of these qualities or traits of man.

6.2. Rational Creatures

Besides the many virtues Locke cites as important for the child to acquire, rationality is perhaps of even greater importance. After his detailed recommendations on how to develop a strong and healthy body, "The next and principle Business is, to set the *Mind* right, that on all Occasions it may be disposed to consent to nothing but what may be suitable to the Dignity and Excellency of a rational Creature".[42] Locke remarks, we all do want to be "thought Rational Creatures".[43] So we must treat children as rational creatures in order that they will come to see the value of rationality.[44] Locke explains that treating children that way involves making them "sensible by the Mildness of your Carriage, and the Composure even in your Correction of them, that what you do is reasonable in you, and useful and necessary for them".[45] The faculty of reason, the operation of reasoning, and being rational all appear in Locke's definitions of man and person.

Whether we believe physical man for Locke includes rationality (the child has to become rational), or whether we think Locke limited rationality to the self or person, what 'flows from' the foundation of man, the inner constitution, includes that property. With the distinction he suggests in one passage between physical and moral man, shape may be the defining feature of the former, rationality and other properties characterize the latter. Whatever properties are included in the definition of man are only those we decide to include or that we find at work in our language. None of these goes beyond what is discovered by experience and observation, but all of these would have some relation to the constitution of man. With physical bodies, both primary and secondary qualities have some relation to the corpuscular structure, but the perceiver or observer plays some role as well in their appearance. There is no such distinction of qualities in Locke's account of man, unless we take the physical man as 'primary' and rational, moral man as 'secondary' or derivative. The 'flow from' relation applies to the properties of both the primary and secondary man. The basic unit is physical man. It is clear that the properties of the person and moral man are also contributions by the man himself, so there may be a double causality in the origin of person-qualities. There may be some question about the strength of Locke's acceptance of the notion of a constitution on which all properties depend. Still, those remarks in *Essay* 3.6.3 are rather unambiguous, if lacking in detail. Locke does not provide us even with a hint about the possible constitution of man, if indeed it differs from the constitution of bodies. But it does seem reasonable for us to suggest that the constitution of the properties of rational man (the secondary sense of 'man') would consist of the particles of the matter of the physical body and, perhaps, the workings of the biological mechanism. How to fit into such a notion the role of the man in the constitution of the person is not clear, but I think we find in Locke's Education the ways in which the child acquires, under the care of parents and the guidance of the tutor, the qualities of a rational person.

6.3. Definition and Theory

What we include in our ideas of physical objects, e.g. iron, gold, lead, is constrained by the qualities we find coexisting together in those objects. Our moral ideas, what Locke calls 'mixed modes', are less tied to what we discover in human action, although they are fairly fixed by the society into which we are born and by that society's language. To use Locke's terminology, mixed-mode ideas are archetypes, determining what counts as parricide, revenge, voting, bidding. Where does the definition of man belong, to mixed modes or to physical objects? It seems more like a mixed mode, depending upon our interest; man is defined in terms of shape (physical man) or in terms of rationality (moral man). Life, sense and, perhaps, solid substance may be included in the definition of physical man; rationality, concern for happiness and misery, acceptance of responsibility for one's actions characterize moral man, or perhaps the self or person.

The reference to the constitution of man from which all those properties flow complicates slightly the question of the definition of man. The similarity with physical substances, a fundamental constitution determining the observed qualities, might suggest that defining man is similar to defining gold or iron: make careful observations of the qualities and characteristics that we find coexisting together. What we include in our definition of gold depends upon our use and interest in that material, but whatever qualities we select must in fact be found to go together. What we mean by 'gold' cannot include properties which experience and experiment cannot find. Experience enlarges our knowledge and understanding of gold or of any other natural substance. In defining man too we cannot impute properties that those we take to be human beings do not have. With physical man, we refer to the body and its inner workings, that man is like any other animal or biological creature—an organization of parts with a common life (*Essay* 3.6.5). A specific shape with sense organs is also found in animals and in man by experience and observation. We do not normally think of humans as a functioning biological body, although of course we recognize that they have such a body, a body necessary for action. As an anthropologist or sociologist, we can observe people in society, noting behavior, speech, accomplishments. To impute traits to those we observe which cannot be found is just as improper as it is to ascribe properties to material bodies that we do not find. Defining man in Locke's project is not, I think, an anthropological task. It is more a matter of unpacking the term 'man' as used in the language and practices of society. At the same time, this enumeration of the ideas contained in the complex idea of man is joined with the theory of a foundation or constitution for the observed features. That theory is not part of the idea of man, it is a feature of Locke's account which is added to the enumeration.

7. Man as Proprietor

In writing about man, person, and self, Locke is not only offering definitions based on the current uses of those terms in his society. He also reveals some of his beliefs about man. The reference to a constitution, from which flow all the observed features and qualities of a man or person, is one such belief. Other beliefs (perhaps they may be stipulative definitions) are provided in his discussion of personal identity, e.g., 'person' is a forensic term, it is the name of the self. There is another belief about man and person Locke held that reveals the special relation he wants to establish between those two: "every Man has a Property in his own Person".[46] This curious notion of owning one's person receives a more interesting expression in a later section of *Two Treatises:* "Man (by being Master of himself and Proprietor of his own Person, and the Actions or Labour of it) had still in himself the great Foundation of Property" (§44). The term 'himself' refers to the man, the little word 'it' refers to the person. The man is the owner of his person, the person acts and labors. As the owner of his person, the man (all men) in the state of nature has the freedom "to order their Actions, and dispose of their Possessions and Person as they think fit", so long as they do so "within the bounds of the Law of Nature" (§4). Section 6 points out that the disposal of his person does not include suicide, the proprietorship of his person is qualified by the law of nature and the ban on taking his own life. The term 'proprietor' is defined in the OED as, "One who holds something as property; one who has the exclusive right or title to the use or disposal of a thing", according to the examples from 1639 and 1645.⁴⁷

The term 'proprietor' is frequently found in a political context, as 'the Lords Proprietors of Carolina', in the Fundamental Constitutions of Carolina (1669), with which Locke was associated. The term occurs frequently in Locke's critique of Robert Filmer in the first of Locke's *Two Treatises* (e.g., §§16, 23, 39, 74, 92). *Essay* 2.12.5 explains the complex idea of theft as "the concealed change of the possession of any thing, without the consent of the Proprietor". Section 120 of the second of *Two Treatises* explains that when a man incorporates himself "into any Commonwealth, he, by his uniting himself thereunto, annexed also, and submits to the Community those Possessions, which he has, or shall acquire". Man in this passage is described as the proprietor of his land; his land and possessions come under the jurisdiction of the government of the community. In uniting with the commonwealth, the man also "unites his Person" to the community. The man's possessions, lands, and person become "subject to the Government and Dominion of that Commonwealth".

In section 44 of *Two Treatises*, Locke does not say that a condition for being the proprietor of his person is being master of himself, but there seems to be an implicit link between mastery and proprietorship of man's person.⁴⁸ To be master of one's self is to have reason as the control of one's desires and passions: that is in part what it is to be a rational creature. To earn the right to own one's person, Locke may be suggesting, we must become rational creatures. Perhaps being rational is being a person. Locke's *Education* is a manual, a set of instructions for parents and tutor to follow in molding the child into a rational, moral person, where mastery of one's self is the goal. Locke's 'Conduct of the Understanding' also speaks of mastery, of the importance of getting mastery over one's understanding and of one's thoughts.⁴⁹ What he says in the *Education* about the mind of the child that is "in tune, and well-disposed" to learning applies equally to the child. The goal is "to teach the

Mind to get the Mastery over itself" (§75). Learning to gain "a Mastery over his [the child's] inclinations" is also one of the tasks assigned to the tutor (§45).

Conclusion

Locke's work on education illustrates his developmental concept of man, of humans. We are in the first instance a material, corporeal, biological organism, the matter of which is composed of corpuscular particles. The difference between this matter and that of substances such as gold or lead is that life and sense have been added. Locke expresses this difference by saying particles of matter are 'vitally' united to our body. He does not offer any explication of that vital union, nor of what makes for the difference between vital and non-vital union. But he does make it clear that the vital union of particles of matter also includes the self, where the self represents the noncorporeal aspect of the live organism. The duality of this vital union of particles, with the body and with the self, indicates Locke's recognition of the tight relation between mind and body.

The treatise on education also reveals his firm conviction of the importance of building specific character traits into the combination of live matter and mind. But he stresses in that work that the child is born with certain tempers or traits. Those native propensities are joined by a general inclination to seek what gratifies and avoid what is distasteful. Besides these inborn features, we are born with specific faculties that are important for later development. That curious suggestion of a constitution of man from which certain operations and qualities 'flow' adds a further native source for man. With these various features, man has a potential for growth, a potential which education (family and society) reinforces, and which the recognition of a life to come, of resurrection and immortality, makes urgent. What is important for immortality (more properly, for accountability) is not a soul; it is the person, the rational, moral, thinking being that each of us owns.[50] We must act in this present world; the acts that count are those that define and characterize the person, moral acts directed by reason, and the laws of nature: God's laws.

So of those four terms with which this chapter began—man, self, person, agent—man turns out to be the central, basic, and most important, man who is self to his self, the agent and appropriator of actions and the proprietor of his person. In identifying man as basic and in some ways more important than the others, we need to guard against treating those terms as referring to separate entities (different Beings). In making distinctions between self and person, or between man, person, and self, there is of course no real separation. A man is a self and a person. Being a person does not involve not being a self, although keeping in mind the developmental features of Locke's account, these may not all occur at the same time in the life of the man. It might be better to talk of different functions of the man, different functionalities, but these would be of the man, not, I think, of physical man, but of man as a conscious, cognitive Being. Later I will suggest some ways in which these component functions can come together to form a single unit, but it is necessary first to take them individually, as I have done in this chapter. Moreover, there is a kind of quiet drama in the development of these components in the *Essay*, a drama that becomes more intense when the soul is introduced.

CHAPTER TWO

THE UNIVERSE AND OUR WORLD

The previous chapter has explored various facets of Locke's man, his secular and moral features. It was important for Locke to show how moral man, the rational person emerges from physical man. The moral component of man, his virtuous conduct, was important for man's social and political life. It was of even greater significance for immortality and the life to come. Locke's man is the workmanship of God; he is one among many other creatures on the chain of being, slightly higher than the beasts and lower than angels and other intelligent Beings. The theological domain of Locke's man now needs to be examined.

Theology for Locke was not a system of doctrines or complex, complicated issues. He characterized theology in his "Conduct" as "containing the Knowledge of God and his Creatures, our Duty to him and our fellow Creatures, and a view of our present and future State" (§22). I suppose the term 'contain' suggests that there is more to theology than the items he lists, but just as his Christianity was minimalist (a belief in Jesus as the Messiah and a few other notions), so the definition of theology is stripped of doctrinal topics. He adds an intriguing remark that links theology to knowledge, or rather, knowledge to theology: theology 'comprehends' "all other Knowledge directed to its true end, i.e. the Honour and Veneration of the

Creator, and the Happiness of Mankind".[1] I understand the term 'comprehend' in this sentence to mean 'include' or 'take in' (one of the *OED*'s definitions). I do not think Locke explains just how theology includes all knowledge, nor does he show how all knowledge leads to the honor and veneration of God and his creatures. Nevertheless, this is an important remark to keep in mind.[2]

The ontological and theological dimensions of Locke's man receive little detailed discussion in the *Essay*, but there is sufficient material to enable us to reconstruct that important aspect of his thought, and there are some direct references which hint at some details. Of the five components of the "Conduct" definition, there is material in the *Essay*, although often only tangential, relevant to (1) our knowledge of God and his creatures, especially (2) our present and future state, (3) a few remarks about our duty to God and his creatures, (4) very little on the honor and veneration of the Creator, and much attention to (5) the happiness of mankind (together, it turns out, with the happiness of God).

One way to view Locke's man is in terms of the different environments to which he belongs, the different contexts that illuminate Locke's understanding of human life. We are familiar from *Two Treatises* and the *Education* with the account Locke gives of man's social context, in the family and in civil society. The bulk of the *Essay* locates man in the immediate physical environment. We have seen how firmly man is rooted in his physical and biological body. The notion of a fundamental constitution of man from which all or most of the physical and moral properties flow would seem to link man, person, and self to neurophysiology, the 'vital union' about which he speaks in several passages. Just how strong this rootedness is, how tied man is to his dependence on the body mechanism, and the ways Locke sees man as the agent of action: all these are important topics for an understanding of Locke's man.

There are three other environments of man in Locke's account; two of these are large, encompassing contexts: the universe itself and the domain of God, Angels and Spirits. A third environment concerns the field of human knowledge and understanding, what Locke refers to as the Intellectual World. This chapter discusses the first and third, chapter 3 takes up the second, which turns out to be another Intellectual World.

1. The Universe

The language Locke employs when referring to the universe is significant for revealing the awe and respect he had for what I assume is the totality of all that exists. The idea of a universe is a complex idea made up of simple ideas (2.12.1). He does not list the simple ideas. The idea of universe is also identified as a collective idea in the brief chapter on collective ideas of substances (2.24.3). There he describes that idea, along with those of 'army' and 'constellation', as artificial, perhaps meaning the referents of those ideas are not really substances, although we treat them as substances. These ideas are "but the artificial Draughts of the Mind, bringing things very remote, and independent on one another, into one view, the better to contemplate, and discourse of them, united into one conception, and signified by one name". The next sentence is especially interesting: "For there are no Things so remote, nor so contrary, which the Mind cannot, by this art of Composition, bring into one *Idea*, as is visible in that signified by the name *Universe*". So the universe is, or our idea of it is, composed of remote and contrary parts.

References to the universe are found throughout the *Essay*, from as early as 2.1.15 to as late as 4.16.12. Various descriptive phrases are employed. For example:

2.2.3: "this vast, and stupendious Universe" and "the Immensity of this Fabrick"

2.23.27: "the Extremities of the Universe"

3.6.9: "the great Fabrick of the Universe"

3.6.12: "the magnificent Harmony of the Universe" (as evidence of the design and goodness of God)

4.6.11: "the great Parts and Wheels ... of this stupendious Structure of the Universe".

(This long, curious section should be read in its entirety, since it gives a striking example of Locke's thinking about the vast universe in which we live. The central thesis of this section is the interconnectedness of all things, objects, animals, and humans: "Things, however absolute and entire they seem in themselves, are but Retainers to other parts of Nature" (4.6.11). The notion of an inner constitution of bodies, or of all the 'things', from which all qualities and properties flow, is replaced here with a much grander notion: "And we in vain search for that Constitution within the Body of a Fly, or an Elephant, upon which depend those Qualities and Powers we observe in them. For which, perhaps, to understand them aright, we ought to look, not only beyond this our Earth and Atmosphere, but even beyond the Sun, or remotest Star our Eyes have yet discovered. For how much the Being and Operation of particular Substances in this our Globe, depend on Causes utterly beyond our view, is impossible for us to determine".)

In his analysis of the idea of place, Locke comments that we can have "no *Idea* of the Place of the Universe, though we can have [an idea] of all the parts of it" (2.13.10). 'Place' is a relative term, so if the universe has a place there would have to be "fixed, distinct, particular Beings, in reference to which, we can imagine it to have any relation of distance". To say "that the World is some where, means no more, than that it does exist".[3] Should someone claim to have a clear, distinct idea of the place of the universe, he would have to "be able to tell us, whether it moves or stands still in the undistinguishable *Inane* of infinite Space". Locke recognizes that "the Word Place has sometimes a more confused Sense, and stands for that Space, which any Body takes up". In this sense, 'the Universe' can be said to be in a place. Does he mean that there is a sense in which the universe can be said to be a body?

The universe is populated with, among other items, bodies, some of which are 'great bodies'.

> 2.13.4: Speaks of the "Bodies of the Universe, or else beyond the utmost Bounds of all Bodies".
>
> 2.13.21 (bis): God can "fix all the Bodies of the Universe in a perfect quiet and rest".
>
> 2.14.22: "the great and visible Bodies of the World" are the measures of time.
>
> 2.14.24: "Beyond the Confines of the World, where are no Bodies at all". (Cf. 2.15.4: "the great *Inane* beyond the Confines of the World". And 2.15.3: "what is beyond the limits of the Universe". Some call this imaginary space. (Cf. 2.15.4.)[4]
>
> 2.14.25: Refers to "the remotest Body of the Universe".
>
> 2.15.3: Speaks of the measure of time "taken from the great Bodies of the World".
>
> 2.15.6: Speaks of the "Motions of the great Bodies of the Universe".
>
> 4.3.24: We are ignorant of the powers of "the greatest part of the Bodies of the Universe". Our ignorance is due to our "not knowing what is the particular *Bulk, Figure,* and *Motion,* of the greatest part of the Bodies of the Universe, we are ignorant of the several Powers, Efficacies, and Ways of Operation, whereby the Effects, which we daily see, are produced".
>
> 4.3.25: "the greatest part of the several ranks of *Bodies* of the Universe, scape our notice by their remoteness". Others do so by their minuteness.

There are a number of references to the matter of the universe.

2.1.15: "the motion of dull and senseless matter, any where in the Universe" (in his discussion of thinking matter).

2.23.27: "For if Matter be considered, as no doubt it is, finite, let any one send his Contemplation to the Extremities of the Universe", and he will not find any forces or bonds that hold matter together. The situation about cohesion is no better if we make the supposition of infinite matter.

4.3.24: "the particular Fabricks of the great Masses of Matter, which make up the whole stupendious frame of Corporeal Beings".

4.10.17: The thinking-matter controversy again. No part of "the Matter of the Universe" can think.

Locke also talks of the parts of the universe, the different 'mansions' of it where creatures or Beings other than humans live.

2.2.3: Refers to "other Mansions of it [the Universe]".

2.14.23: The chapter on duration and time. He refers to other parts of the universe where other measures than inches and feet may be used. He mentions Japan as one place that uses other measures, but the "other parts of the Universe" seems to include other places, other countries perhaps although he does not speak of countries.

2.23.12: Speaks of our "well-being in this part of the Universe, which we inhabit".

4.10.7: Refers to "the sensible parts of the Universe", so I assume there are non-sensible parts. Whether these are just parts of the physical universe not available to us through sense perception, or whether the non-sensible parts are or include intellectual, spiritual, or immaterial parts is not clear. Later, I will ask, is what I call the domain of God, Angels and Spirits part of the universe? If so, that domain would be a non-sensible, immaterial part.[5]

> 4.16.12: Speaks of "Plants, Animals, and intelligent Inhabitants in the Planets, and other Mansions of the vast Universe".

At best, these few statements give us the outlines of some aspects of the universe as conceived by Locke. Late in the *Essay* he remarks that we are "far from being able to comprehend the whole nature of the Universe, and all the things contained in it" (4.3.29). Whether we can say he comprehended certain aspects of the universe, we can at least summarize what he says about it. It exists, it is vast and immense, it has a structure made up of masses of matter, it has outer boundaries, its parts are in harmony, it is not in a place but all its component parts (the corporeal parts?) are, some parts are inhabited by Beings other than and different from ourselves, and it was created and had a beginning. This last listed feature appears when he discusses the idea of duration in 2.14.24–30 and also in 2.15.7. In these sections, Locke offers an analysis of how we form ideas of duration, even extending those ideas back to the beginning before there was any motion or bodies to serve as the measures of time. In that way, he explains, "I can imagine that Light existed three days before the Sun was, or had any motion" (2.14.30). He does that "by thinking, that the duration of Light before the Sun was created, was so long as (if the Sun had moved then, as it doth now,) would have been equal to three of his diurnal Revolutions". Of even more interest, "by the same way I can have an *Idea* of the *Chaos*, or Angels, being created before there was either Light, or any continued motion, a Minute, an Hour, a Day, a Year, or 1000 Years".[6]

Locke recognized that in saying the world had a beginning he was begging the question, "That the World is neither eternal, nor infinite" (2.14.26). He replies that "to my present purpose, it is not needful, in this place, to make use of Arguments, to evince the World to be finite, both in Duration and Extension". He thinks it is equally conceivable to say the world is finite or to say it is eternal. I am assuming that the world is the same as the universe in these passages. That is not always the case.

Whether the universe is finite or infinite, man occupies a small part of the stupendous totality. In "this Globe of Earth alotted for our Mansion, the all-wise Architect has suited our Organs, and the Bodies, that are to affect them, one to another" (2.23.12). The analyses of sensation and perception, the formation of ideas, the extent and limits of human knowledge, the explication of specific ideas such as space, time, solidity: these and much else in the *Essay* give us Locke's account of the interrelations of bodily organs and external objects. There are, of course, other topics discussed. But besides these specific topics, Locke also provides us with an overview of human knowledge, a schema for organizing the areas or, to use his term, 'provinces'.

2. The Intellectual World as Our World

The very last section of Locke's *Essay* identifies "the three great Provinces of the intellectual World", those provinces being "wholly separate and distinct one from another" (4.21.5). The use of the term 'provinces' indicates the territory or area addressed by what Locke calls 'intellectual Beings', the subject matter of their interests and investigations. Those provinces concern (1) "*Things* as they are in themselves knowable", (2) "*Actions* as they depend on us, in order to Happiness", and (3) "the right use of *Signs* in order to Knowledge". The title of this final chapter is "Of the Division of the Sciences", where he distinguishes three: natural philosophy, ethics, and the doctrine of signs. The three provinces 'contain' things, actions, and signs. The three sciences are the study of things, actions, and signs. In this usage, science means 'systematic investigation'. The provinces may be distinct and separate, but the items in those provinces have some relations with each other. Human actions involve the body and they take place in the realm of things, of physical objects and events. Some signs, verbal ones, have physical forms, and they are used to talk about things and actions. In other words, the three sciences are directed towards the contents of the three provinces.[7]

2.1. Natural Philosophy as Speculation

The three-fold division of provinces and sciences encompasses all that falls within our understanding, all that can be known, believed, prescribed, and expressed. Ethics and moral theory were common topics in the seventeenth and eighteenth centuries. Signs, even doctrines of signs, can be found in late scholastic writings, but Locke's use of the notion of signs (both ideas and words) stands out from that of his contemporaries. The one science that he modified is natural philosophy. For him the scope of natural philosophy is rather broad: "The Knowledge of Things, as they are in their own proper Beings, their Constitutions, Properties, and Operations" (4.21.2). He is careful to say that natural philosophy includes (and here is where he modifies that science) "not only Matter, and Body, but Spirits also, which have their proper Natures, Constitutions, and Operations". That he considered this definition different from the usual is indicated by his calling it an 'enlarged sense' of the term, and his repetition in the same paragraph of the 'things' that are included in natural philosophy: the end or goal of natural philosophy "is bare speculative Truth, and whatsoever can afford the Mind of Man any such, falls under this branch, whether it be God himself, Angels, Spirits, Bodies, or any of their Affections, as Number, and Figure, *etc.*"[8]

Several parts of this statement need attention. First is the identification of the goal of natural philosophy as speculative truth. Perhaps the contrast is with empirical truth, but the meaning of 'truth' seems rather different in these two uses. We can speculate about God, Angels and Spirits, but there seems to be no way for us to know whether our speculations are true. The concept of speculative truth is not clear. Second, the inclusion of bodies as objects of speculative truth is rather odd, especially since Locke spends much of the *Essay* on ways to discover some truths about bodies. Of course, he does so by distinguishing what we can observe about bodies from their inner nature and constitution. The third part of Locke's definition or description of natural philosophy that we should query is the phrase 'in themselves knowable'. God, Angels and Spirits generally must be among the things studied in the first of the three provinces of the intellectual world, but do they fit the description of things "in themselves knowable"? Not, I think, without some specification of his understanding of 'knowable', which would cover bodies and spirits. Speculative truth applies not only to spirits: when we try to determine the constitution of bodies, and their causal powers, observation does not reveal their 'proper being'. Locke accepts the corpuscular theory as a useful hypothesis (speculation), but our knowledge of body is limited to experience and observation. Natural philosophy is larger in scope than the science of nature he so carefully described earlier in the *Essay*; that science, an experimental science, is restricted to experience and does not allow for speculation. Perhaps experimental science is part of natural philosophy, but the text is unclear on their relation. The lack of clarity stems from the fact that natural philosophy is said to concern the constitution, properties, and operations of bodies in their own proper beings, since he was skeptical about our being able to go beyond what we can discover by experience.[9] However, Locke does not hesitate to suggest what the result would be were we able to uncover the inner constitution of bodies: we would have an a priori science, not an experimental one.

The experimental science of nature concerned what Locke calls the material world or the sensible world. The material world (2.15.6; 3.10.22) refers to the space-time world of physical objects and events. The sensible world (2.15.6,8; 4.3.23) refers to those aspects of the material world available to us, to sensible beings. His *Essays on the Law of Nature* has a rather comprehensive list of what is available to us in sense experience:

> In the first place, then, we say it is evident from sense-experience that in the natural world there are perceptible objects, i.e. that there really exist solid bodies and their conditions, namely lightness and heaviness, warmth and coldness, colours and the rest of the qualities presented to the senses, which can all in some way be traced back to

motion; that this visible world is constructed with wonderful art and regularity, and of this world we, the human race, are also a part. We certainly see the stars turning round in an unbroken and fixed course, rivers rolling along into the sea, and the years and changes of the seasons following one another in a definite order. This and almost infinitely more we learn from the senses. (p. 151)

The sensible world is a sub-set of the material world, all that we can discover about the material world by experience and observation. 'World' in this usage differs from its use in 'intellectual world'. The latter is or concerns the ideas, beliefs, theories, and conjectures we have about the material world. Manipulating and experimenting with objects in the material world differs from our dealings with thoughts and disputes about the objects and events in the material world. The world of ideas differs from the world of bodies. This distinction is found in 2.12.1 of the *Essay*. After describing complex ideas, where the mind is passive in the reception of ideas but active in comparing or abstracting them, Locke asserts that "Man's Power and its [the mind's ?] way of Operation . . . [is] muchwhat the same in the Material and Intellectual World. For the Materials in both being such as he has no power over, either to make or destroy, all that Man can do is either to unite them together, or to set them by one another, or wholly separate them". The components of the material world are bits of matter, physical events. The materials of the intellectual world are ideas. We cannot make or destroy simple ideas; we can only receive them, compare them, combine them, etc. He makes a similar comparison earlier: "The Dominion of Man, in this little World of his own Understanding, being muchwhat the same, as it is in the great World of visible things; wherein his Power, however managed by Art and Skill, reaches no farther, than to compound and divide the Materials, that are made to his Hand; can do nothing towards the making the least Particle of new Matter, or destroying one Atome of what is already in Being" (2.2.2). The same, he continues, is true of our trying to make a new simple idea "not received ... from external Objects, or by reflection from the Operation of his own mind about them".

A later section on the limits and extent of knowledge makes a similar comparison between the intellectual world and the sensible world, but there he seems to introduce a different kind of intellectual world: he remarks that "the intellectual and sensible World, are in this perfectly alike; That that part, which we see of either of them, holds no proportion with what we see not; And whatsoever we can reach with our Eyes, or our Thoughts of either of them, is but a point, almost nothing, in comparison of the rest" (4.3.23). If the intellectual world is the world of ideas, what sense can we give to the notion that there are parts of it not available to us? That is the section where Locke talks of other spirits, other intellectual beings, which are beyond our senses. The intellectual world now seems to be identified with the realm of these other Beings. Our eyes cannot reach them, perhaps our thoughts can. It would be useful to know how thought reaches (conjectures, reasons, speculates) features of what little of either world we can access.

Later in the same chapter, he seems to return to the other sense of intellectual world, the world of ordinary thoughts, beliefs, and ideas. Bemoaning the endless disputes and debates often marked by not paying close attention to the words men use, becoming lost in the "great Wood of Words" (4.3.30), Locke seems to assign such logomachy to that intellectual world. He contrasts this weakness of the intellectual world with the solid achievements made in the material world.

> Had Men, in the discoveries of the material, done, as they have in those of the intellectual World, involved all in the obscurity of uncertain and doubtful ways of talking, Volumes writ of Navigation and Voyages, Theories and Stories of Zones and Tydes multiplied and disputed; nay, Ships built, and Fleets set out, would never have taught us the way beyond the Line; and the Antipodes would be still as much unknown, as when it was declared Heresy to hold there were any. (4.3.30)

The chapter on the abuse of words gives us a detailed diagnosis of the ills that can and have infected many participants in the intellectual world (3.10.22). One passage in section 22 of that chapter summarizes the disease:

> The multiplication and obstinacy of Disputes, which has so laid waste the intellectual World, is owing to nothing more, than to this ill use of Words. For though it be generally believed, that there is a great diversity of Opinions in the Volumes and Variety of Controversies, the World is distracted with; yet the most I can find, that the contending learned Men of different Parties do, in their Arguings one with another, is, that they speak different Languages.

Locke's man belongs to both the material and the intellectual worlds. Men are described in one passage as "intellectual corporeal Beings" (4.3.24). It is one and the same intellectual being who gets lost in the wood of words but who also makes informative and useful discoveries about the material world, at least so much of that world that is available to us. Much of the *Essay* and the 'Conduct of the Understanding' are concerned with ways to enable man, the intellectual corporeal being, to avoid the verbal and conceptual puzzlements that characterized the writings and thinking of some of Locke's contemporaries and predecessors, especially in relation to the material world—the world of matter and physical bodies. A change of methodology is the remedy, a change from following tradition, accepting the views of others, to careful observation and a precise use of words. That alteration in the method of enquiry takes place in Locke's intellectual world, but it has consequences in the material world, consequences for knowledge and in the use of objects. If we take seriously Locke's definition of natural philosophy at the end of the *Essay*, that it uses the method of speculative truth not only when dealing with spirits but also when directed towards bodies, then the difference between natural philosophy and Locke's experimental science of nature is marked indeed: it is the difference between speculative truth and empirical truth. The science of nature is conducted by scientists such as Boyle or Sydenham; in the *Essay*, Locke is engaged in natural philosophy.

2.2. Conjecture as Method

I remarked above that the concept of speculative truth is not clear. We also saw Locke's suggestion of a distinction between what our eyes can 'reach' (discover?) and what our thoughts can 'reach'. I suggested the latter notion might include conjecture as a way of 'reaching' what our eyes and sense experience cannot discover about the objects of Locke's enlarged natural philosophy. Speculation about the material world and about the world of God, Angels and Spirits may consist in making conjectures or even guesses about the nature and operations of those Beings.

The chapter in the *Essay* on probability comments on the limits of our knowledge and our inability "to find certain Truth in every thing which we have occasion to consider" (4.15.2). Moreover, "most of the Propositions we think, reason, discourse, nay act upon, are such, as we cannot have undoubted Knowledge of their Truth: yet some of them border so near upon Certainty, that we make no doubt at all about them; but *assent* to them as firmly, and act, according to that Assent, as resolutely, as if they were infallibly demonstrated, and that our Knowledge of them was perfect and certain". He then lists degrees from certainty and demonstration "quite down to Improbability and Unlikeliness, even to the Confines of Impossibility". There are also degrees of assent, a very important function for Locke, "from full *Assurance* and Confidence, quite down to *Conjecture, Doubt,* and *Distrust*". The chapter on degrees of assent (4.16) elaborates on this notion. Section 9 of that chapter offers another list: "*Belief, Conjecture, Guess, Doubt, Wavering, Distrust, Disbelief*". In the first list, conjecture is located between confidence and doubt, in the second list it comes right after belief and ahead of guess.

There are not many guesses in the *Essay*. Locke does suggest that a man "accustomed to rational and regular Experiments shall be able to see farther into the Nature of Bodies, and guess righter at their yet unknown Properties" (4.12.10). Such a guess would be an informed one, based on past experience by those involved in experimental science. Even scientists, and especially most of us, are unable to guess what effects the minute parts of animals and plants will produce; we can only observe and record what does occur (4.3.26). But Locke does suggest that by analogy we may be able to guess what the effects will be of similar bodies in similar situations (4.3.6). Invoking the principle that all ideas have their first rise in sense, he suggests that we may be able to guess "what kind of Notions they were, and whence derived, which filled their Minds, who were the first Beginners of Languages" (3.1.5). He also allows that where we fail to perceive the agreement or disagreement of ideas (his definition of knowledge), "we may fancy, guess or believe" but we will come short of knowledge (4.1.2). As regards spirits, "we may guess at some part of the Happiness of superior Ranks of Spirits" (4.3.6), but we cannot guess at "what sorts of Furniture and Inhabitants those Mansions [other mansions of the universe] contain" (4.3.24). So I think we can dismiss guessing as a mode of speculation, certainly not a significant component. Much more likely is conjecture.

There are a number of passages where Locke explicitly offers a conjecture. For example, in 2.9.5 he suggests that children in the womb have ideas of hunger and warmth. He adds, "if one may conjecture concerning things not very capable of examination". In section 15 of this chapter, he offers as his conjecture that perception in the lowest degree marks the boundaries "between Animals, and the inferior ranks of Creatures". In 2.11.15, he conjectures that beasts do not have general ideas and hence do not engage in abstract reasoning. He makes what he labels an 'odd conjecture' in 2.14.9, that "There seem to be *certain Bounds to the quickness or Slowness of the Succession of* those *Ideas* one to another in our Minds, beyond which they can neither delay nor hasten" (2.14.9).[10] He does offer a fascinating basis in experience for this conjecture: "Let a Cannon-Bullet pass through a Room, and in its way take with it any Limb, or fleshy Parts of a Man; 'tis as clear as any Demonstration can be, that it must strike successively the two sides of the Room: 'Tis also evident, that it must touch one part of the Flesh first, and another after; and so in Succession: And yet I believe, no Body, who ever felt the pain of such a shot, or heard the blow against the two distant Walls, could perceive any Succession, either in the pain, or sound of so swift a stroke" (2.14.10). Later in the *Essay* he remarks that the mind does not always perceive the agreement or disagreement of ideas, "even when it is discoverable". In this case, the mind "remains in Ignorance, and at most, gets no farther than a probable conjecture" (4.2.2).

Two of these examples concern the acquisition of ideas, their perception and succession. Another relates to Locke's interest in boundaries between species, not the fixed boundaries of those who held to the notion of real essences which determine species, but in Locke's nominal essence sense of observed coexisting qualities. A related example of conjecture is found in his discussion in the chapter on the improvement of knowledge. There he points out that since we do not know the real essence of any substance, we are unable to know in advance of experience what qualities will coexist in the future. He suggests that we might conjecture about what will occur next, but he does not recommend doing so—experience and observation are what we should rely upon (4.12.9). Later, he emphasizes, in 4.16.12, that we can only conjecture about the causes of what we experience and observe; we do not have a knowledge of those causes.

Perhaps the most interesting example of conjecture to be found in the *Essay* is in 4.12.13 where he mentions hypotheses that are used to explain phenomena. He warns against an uncritical acceptance of hypotheses, because they may just be doubtful conjectures, adding, "such as are most (I had almost said all) of the *Hypotheses* in natural Philosophy".[11]

2.3. Examples of Natural Philosophy

If we search in the *Essay* for references to natural philosophy, will they be to the enlarged sense that was described in 4.21, dealing with spirits as well as with bodies? One passage may reflect that sense of natural philosophy, although in this passage Locke is being critical. He is discussing the use of trifling propositions that are passed off as knowledge. "Demonstrations and undoubted Propositions" can be produced without advancing knowledge at all (4.8.9). He lists a string of terms that have been used in this way: substance, man, animal, form, soul, vegetative, rational. A man may "make several undoubted Propositions about the Soul, without knowing at all what the Soul really is". He goes on to say, "and of this sort, a Man may find an infinite number of Propositions, Reasonings, and Conclusions, in Books of Metaphysicks, School-Divinity, and some sort of natural Philosophy; and after all, know as little of GOD, *Spirits*, or *Bodies*, as he did before he set out". The phrase 'some sort of natural Philosophy' is a reference to bad metaphysics and natural philosophy, but this passage may be seen as another use of that enlarged sense of natural philosophy.[12] Trifling propositions no more yield knowledge in natural philosophy than in any other field. Identical propositions, e.g., *"a Soul is a Soul"; a Spirit is a Spirit"*, are examples of trifling propositions. Such propositions are equivalent to saying *"What is, is"*, or *"what hath existence hath existence'* (4.8.3). Other examples are given in subsequent sections. Such propositions are clearly not instructive and carry no information. There are other non-trivial propositions in natural philosophy, such as *"two Bodies cannot be in the same place"*. Locke offers this proposition as an example of those that produce immediate assent, but they are not innate, as some claimed (1.2.18).

The use of maxims is similarly rejected as a means to truth and knowledge. Natural philosophy is mentioned again in this context (4.12.4). Locke queries whether knowledge can be obtained by beginning "with general Maxims, and build[ing] upon them", or whether it is helpful to take "the *Principles,* which are laid down in any other Science, as unquestionable Truths" without any examination or testing of those principles. To employ such a reliance on maxims and unexamined principles could produce results that might appear as truths in natural philosophy.

> He that shall consider, *how little general Maxims, precarious Principles, and Hypotheses laid down at Pleasure, have promoted true Knowledge,* or helped to satisfy the Enquiries of rational Men after real Improvements; How little, I say, the setting out at the end, has for many Ages together advanced Men's Progress towards the Knowledge of natural Philosophy, will think, we have Reason to thank those, who in this latter Age have taken another Course, and have trod out to us, though not an easier way to learned Ignorance, yet a surer way to profitable Knowledge. (4.12.12)

The surer way to useful knowledge is to employ experience and observation. Prior to this passage, Locke said that he 'suspects' that "natural Philosophy is not capable of being made a Science" (4.12.10), but the science there was a demonstrative, certain science based on a discovery of the essence or inner constitution of body.[13] This remark occurs within a series of sections in which he both praised the new science of experience and observation and seems to lament its limitations. 'Learned ignorance' and 'profitable', i.e., useful, practical knowledge, is his characterization of the results of that science. "This *way* of getting, and *improving our Knowledge in Substances only by Experience* and History, which is all the weakness of our Faculties in this State of *Mediocrity,* which we are in in this World, can attain to" (4.12.10). Were we able to turn natural philosophy into a science, what would be required is a discovery of the real essence, the inner constitution of various substances. Then we would have certain knowledge of all the properties that 'flow from' that constitution: "from a Discovery of their real Essences, [we would be able to] grasp at a time whole Sheaves; and in bundles, comprehend the Nature and Properties of whole Species together" (4.12.12). Our "Faculties are not fitted to penetrate into the internal Fabrick and real Essences of Bodies" (4.12.11). It is as if Locke wants natural philosophy to approach as closely as possible to the certain knowledge that real essences would provide. Section 14 of this chapter speaks of ways to "enlarge our Knowledge", i.e. by endeavoring to make our ideas as complete as possible and, more importantly, to make our ideas clear and distinct. He refers to co-existing ideas (qualities), so there seems to be a reference to experimental natural philosophy. His final remark in this paragraph is that our ideas are "either imperfect, confused, or obscure, [so] we cannot expect to have certain, perfect, or clear Knowledge". In his *Education*, Locke describes natural philosophy as "a speculative Science", adding: "I imagin we have none, and perhaps, I may think I have reason to say, we never shall be able to make a Science of it". His reason is our lack of sufficient knowledge which would enable us to 'reduce' it to a science.[14]

One other passage in the *Essay* where natural philosophy is mentioned is worth attention. In stressing the need for clarity in the use of words, making sure that the ideas they stand for are clear, Locke cites, as examples of those who fail to link ideas to words, "the great Mint-Masters of these kind of Terms, I mean the Schoolmen and Metaphysicians, (under which, I think, the disputing natural and moral Philosophers of these latter Ages, may be comprehended)" (3.10.2). Clear definitions are required in moral and natural philosophy.

In this passage, natural philosophy is grouped with the non-instructive methods and claims of much traditional philosophy. Locke wanted to replace that method with knowledge-inducing procedures. But that 4.21.2 section seems to suggest a more positive, useful natural philosophy. Locke does not seem to want to eliminate natural philosophy, only the bad kind. Some evidence for this suggestion may be found in his discussion of science education for children. He refers to "abstruse Speculations of Natural Philosophy, and Metaphysics", warning that rather than fill the heads of a son with these, it is better to equip him with practical knowledge.[15] The same point is made later in this section: no one should expect a young gentleman to "Go to the bottom of Metaphysicks, Natural Philosophy or Mathematics".[16] Nevertheless, "It is necessary for a Gentleman in this learned Age to look into some of them, to fit himself for Conversation".[17] At least the young man should examine the hypotheses in some of the systems of natural philosophy. Just how much value Locke thinks there is in some traditional systems of natural philosophy, these few remarks in the Education may not reveal, but I think we can say that along with his experimental science of nature, *Essay* 4.21.2 seems to suggest the value of a good natural philosophy.

One example of a useful natural philosophy concerning bodies is Locke's use of neurophysiology to explain the experience of one hand feeling hot, another cold, when both are placed in the same water (2.8.21). He uses the same physiology in his consideration of the possibility of a mechanical (neurophysiological) cause of a bird's singing. (2.10.10).[18] The physiology is the standard animal spirit physiology, which was generally accepted then.[19] The importance of this passage lies not in that particular type of physiology, but just in the fact that he goes beyond experience to offer a conjecture, an hypothesis, to account for a specific experience. Phenomena are explained by reference to underlying causal processes. He describes this explanation as a "little Excursion into Natural Philosophy" (2.8.22). The second section of chapter 1, book 1 characterizes such an excursion into the physiology behind mental processes as 'speculation', confirming his expanded meaning of natural philosophy: "I shall not at present meddle with the Physical Consideration of the Mind; or trouble my self to examine, wherein its Essence consists, or by what Motions of our Spirits [animal spirits], or Alterations of our Bodies, we come to have any Sensation by our Organs, or any *Ideas* in our Understandings; and whether those *Ideas* do in their Formation, any, or all of them, depend on Matter, or no. These are Speculations . . .". Another example of his use of natural philosophy concerning the body is his acceptance of the corpuscular theory of matter.

2.4. Immaterial Principles and Immaterial Powers

Locke's acceptance of the great chain of being can be viewed as natural philosophy in his enlarged sense concerning spirits, the many Beings up and down the chain, especially those above us. In the *Education* he offers an interesting reason for studying spirits: "For without the notion and allowance of Spirits, our Philosophy will be lame and defective in one main Part of it, when it leaves out the Contemplation of the most Excellent and Powerful Part of the Creation" (§190). In recommending "a good History of the Bible, for young People to read", selections from the Bible suitable for the young, Locke explains that in reading such a book "there would be instilled into the Minds of Children, a notion and belief of Spirits, they [spirits] having so much to do in all the Transactions of that History" (§190).[20] The result would be "a good Preparation to the study of Bodies". He elaborates this remark in section 192: "Matter being a thing, that all our Senses are constantly conversant with, it is so apt to possess the Mind, and exclude all other Beings, but Matter, that prejudice, grounded on such Principles, often leaves no room for the admittance of Spirits, or the allowing any such things as *immaterial Beings in rerum natura*".[21] He rejects the notion that the "great Phænomena of Nature" can be adequately explained by reference to matter and motion, citing gravity as a phenomenon in need of immaterial principles. By 'principles', he really means 'cause' or 'power'. It is "the positive Will of a Superiour Being, so ordering it" that gravity has the effects it does (§192). He even offers an explanation of Noah's flood: "God's altering the Center of gravity in the Earth for a time". The active intervention of God in nature, God being immaterial, is what Locke has in mind. It is not only God, but other spirits that are immaterial and have powers to intervene in nature: "the necessity of having recourse to something beyond bare Matter and its Motion, in the explication of Nature; to which the Notions of Spirits and their Power, as deliver'd in the Bible, where so much is attributed to their Operation, may be a fit Preparative" for a young gentleman (§192).

The appeal to immaterial principles and powers in these sections of the *Education* concerns special intervention in the 'great phenomena' of nature.[22] We might wonder whether Locke would extend the need for immaterial principles and powers to lesser phenomena, e.g., human thought and action? The intervention of God and other spirits in such phenomena as our deliberating, choosing, deciding, and acting, or even of the movement of arms and legs in walking, is not something Locke would entertain. Some of his contemporaries, e.g., Malebranche, did have God taking an active role in such actions. But God and other spirits are not the only immaterial causes and powers in Locke's account. The mind itself is immaterial, as is also the soul (assuming some difference between them), and both are active causes in human life. Just as the singing of birds cannot be explained by mechanical, physical causes (they must have ideas as patterns), so man forms ideas and employs mental faculties and powers in thinking and acting. The endorsement of immaterial principles and powers in the passage from *Education* is not directed towards human thought and actions. There, Locke addresses the context of large-scale physical phenomena. The actions of God and spirits do not take away man's freedom or man's power.

3. A Second Intellectual World

One of the more curious remarks in these sections of the *Education* is Locke's claim that the study of spirits coming before the study of matter and bodies will enlarge "our Minds towards a truer and fuller comprehension of the Intellectual World", a world "to which we are led both by Reason and Revelation" (§190). Here is the second sense of intellectual world: it applies to that segment of the chain of being above man's location. This same restriction of the intellectual world to the realm of spirits is found in the *Essay* (4.3.27). The prior section makes the point that we have "no *Ideas* of the particular mechanical Affections of the minute parts of Bodies, that are within our view and reach, we are ignorant of their Constitutions, Powers, and Operations: and of Bodies more remote, we are yet more ignorant not knowing so much as their very outward Shapes or the sensible and grosser parts of their Constitutions". Section 27 speaks about our lack of knowledge of "that infinite number of *Spirits* that may be, and probably" do exist. These are beyond our comprehension, we are unable to "frame to our selves any distinct *Ideas* of their several ranks and sorts". Thus, "almost the whole intellectual World" is concealed from us "in an impenetrable obscurity". That intellectual world is "a greater certainly, and more beautiful World, than the material".

So both the *Education* passage and the *Essay* 4.3.27 passage clearly use the phrase 'intellectual world' to refer to the domain of spirits.[23] There is some similar language in three passages in his "Conduct" where the reference is not so clear. Since the "Conduct" was originally planned for a chapter in the *Essay*, it is not surprising to find similar language and the same topics. One passage speaks of the importance of giving the mind "a fair and equal view of the whole intellectual World, wherein it may see the Order, Rank, and Beauty of the whole, and give a just allowance to the distinct Provinces of the several Sciences, in the due Order and Usefulness of each of them" (§18, p. 59). The reference to 'provinces' surely links this passage with the *Essay*'s 4.21.5 talk of three provinces available to us, so this passage would seem to use 'intellectual world' in the first sense: it is not a reference to the domain of God, Angels and Spirits. The ascription of beauty to this world, as with the ascription in those sections just cited where the intellectual world is clearly the domain of God, Angels and Spirits, adds a puzzle to our understanding. The second 'Conduct' passage also talks of 'beautiful provinces'. Locke speaks of those of limited knowledge, cooped up "within narrow Bounds", not "looking abroad into other Provinces of the intellectual World", a world "more beautiful possibly, and more fruitful" than those of narrow bounds (§21, p. 65). The third passage also seems to be consistent with the other two: "God has made the intellectual World Harmonious and Beautiful without us; but it will never come into our Heads all at once, we must bring it home Piece-meal" (§37, p. 110). Just how we can bring the world into our heads is not entirely clear, but I suppose it refers in part to our method of discovery by experience and observation. We learn about the material world in this way, and we grow up in family and society, so we acquire some knowledge of personal and social relations. If we take 'intellectual world' in these 'Conduct' passages to be the same as that described in *Essay* 4.21.5, then I assume we gradually discover in a piece-meal fashion the items in those three provinces: natural philosophy, ethics, and the nature and role of words (language) and ideas. If natural philosophy extends to speculation about other spirits, then perhaps these 'Conduct' passages are meant to apply to both intellectual worlds.

I said the inclusion of beauty among the features of the intellectual world is puzzling; at least, it adds a bit of uncertainty as to what Locke intends. It may be that all Locke intends is the not unfamiliar reference to the "order, harmony, and beauty which is to be found in Nature", as he says in *Essay* 4.10.10. I suspect beauty in this context is the same as the order and harmony of the 'stupendious universe' in which we are situated. We have some idea of the order and harmony of the planets and stars. Where our comprehension fails is in the attempt to frame some understanding of the order, harmony, and beauty of the domain of God, Angels and Spirits.[24]

Whether we can understand the ascription of beauty to both uses of the intellectual world concept, there are several important aspects of these passages from the *Education*, the "Conduct", and the *Essay*. Besides the explicit restriction in several of the passages of the intellectual world to the realm of spirit, we find a firm assertion of the need for non-material principles. There is a strong rejection of materialism, of matter and motion. In the sections of the *Education*, he also says that reason and revelation lead us to the notion of that restricted intellectual world, and that revelation, not speculation, gives us information about the spirits or Beings that inhabit that world. However, speculation may still have a role. What he says is that "the clearest and largest Discoveries we have of other Spirits, besides God, and our own Souls, is imparted to us from Heaven, by Revelation" (§190). Just what speculation provides is not specified in that passage. Some of Locke's account of the Beings on the chain of being may involve speculation. Notice also in this last remark, the listing of the human soul as part of that restricted intellectual world, one of the spirits, I assume, on the chain.

Conclusion

Perhaps it is not quite clear where the human soul is located in Locke's account. Nor is his commitment to the notion of soul unambiguous. The soul in this last passage is grouped with non-material (immaterial) items on the chain or scale of being. The soul of man seems to occupy two domains, the material domain while linked with the body, the restricted intellectual world when the body is dissolved. However, what is resurrected according to Locke's account, is the person, albeit with some bodily form. He also suggests that immateriality was not necessary for immortality. If immateriality is not necessary, does this mean a soul is not required? Could he possibly mean that a material soul is consistent with immortality? Locke's critics in the seventeenth century understood that his rejection of immateriality as necessary for immortality was a rejection of the soul. He insisted that he did not reject the soul, but did he mean to suggest that the soul is not necessary for immortality? That would indeed be a radical doctrine. Can he separate immateriality from the soul? Is there some implication about the nature and location of the soul in his insistence that a soul, if indeed this is what he meant, is not required for immortality? It is difficult to know what if any implication is involved—Locke is rather silent on this theological question, at least in the *Essay*. However, if the soul is one of the spirits on the chain, as he says in the *Education*, and as we shall discover this feature of the soul is elaborated in the *Essay*, the soul gets reinstated and plays a prominent role in immortality.

CHAPTER THREE

THE WORLD OF GOD, ANGELS, AND SPIRITS

As we have seen, Locke invokes two notions of the intellectual world, one in *Essay* 4.21.5, which we might label the epistemological sense of that notion. This is the world of investigations into the nature and extent of our knowledge of the material world, as well as the examination of the understanding, which is the subject-matter of much of the *Essay*. The epistemological sense also involves an analysis of human action, its motives, its freedom, and responsibility—concepts that play an important role in the account of moral action and personhood. A third component of this sense of the intellectual world is the doctrine of signs, the ways of communication available to us, the need for clarity and precise definitions. These are also the subject-matter of much of the *Essay*.

The second notion of the intellectual world is that of a special domain, a non-material domain. Perhaps we could label this the ontological sense. Here, Locke is not concerned with human knowledge, action, or communication. This intellectual world is paired and contrasted with the material world, the world or domain of physical processes, external objects. What is interesting about these two domains is the awe and aesthetic attitude towards the immaterial domain Locke expressed, the domain of God, Angels and other Spirits. It is also of some interest to see the creatures and beings that inhabit both domains, domains that I assume constitute the universe.

1. Creatures, Beings and Spirits

1.1. Creatures

Locke employs the three terms in this section heading, sometimes with added labels, to describe and comment on the inhabitants of both domains. He tends to use the term 'creature' especially for members of the material domain and for those (i.e., humans) who use the epistemological sense of 'intellectual world', but there are some important occurrences of that term for other creatures above us on the chain. That term is also used to characterize general words and mixed modes, as creatures of our understanding (3.3.11; 3.5.5; 3.11.20; 4.18.3). Other uses are for plants and their products (2.3.2; 2.32.22, 23). A larger group of creatures are animals. For example, speaking of "the infinite wise Creator of us, and all things about us", Locke remarks that we have sufficient faculties to "discover enough in the Creatures, to lead us to the Knowledge of the Creator" (2.23.12). For other references to animals as creatures see 2.7.5; 3.6.27; 4.6.11.

The more interesting uses of the term 'creature' are those applied to man and other Beings on the chain of being. The 2.2.3 passage that says it is not impossible for God to make a creature with other sense organs than those we have also contains a reference to intelligent Beings in other parts of the universe. Creatures fall into ranks and come in degrees (2.8.12). Some ranks are inferior to others; man probably being an example of an inferior rank (2.9.15). The section in which he lays out the doctrine of the chain of being explicitly speaks of "the *Species* of Creatures" that by "gentle degrees, ascend upward from us toward infinite Perfection" (3.6.12). There are also some that descend from us, but there are many more above than below us. *Essay* 2.8.15 remarks on the relation between numbers of sense organs and amount of knowledge, a remark applied to "any Man, as well as other Creatures". We are only finite creatures (2.21.49); the next section describes us as "short-sighted Creatures".[1] *Essay* 2.23.13 repeats the suggestion that God could make creatures with other faculties and ways of perceiving (cf. 3.6.4; 4.3.23; and 4.12.3). When we say "the Creatures are all weak Things", Locke explains that the term 'weak' is "a relative term, signifying the disproportion there is in the Power of GOD, and the Creatures" (2.26.6). 'Rational creatures' is a term found frequently in other sections (e.g., 3.6.9; 4.10.8; 4.12.11; 4.18.11) and in other of Locke's books.[2]

The chain of being is detailed in 3.6.12, and the detail is carried on in section 22 of that chapter where a rather important remark is made. He refers to the "internal real Constitution" of some creatures, a constitution from which flow all other properties. As we have seen in chapter 1, he also claims the same notion of an internal constitution for man, and it was an important part of his account of material bodies, even though in none of these cases is that a knowledge we can acquire. This feature of an internal constitution thus seems to be a fundamental feature of all creatures and Beings on the chain.

The frequent use of the term 'creatures' reflects Locke's religious orientation even in a work on the understanding. There is an especially interesting passage where creatures are used in Locke's critique of the traditional doctrine of essence, a fundamental feature of the *Essay*, the notion that there are fixed kinds, each kind having its own defining essence. In this passage, changelings are the creatures being discussed. Locke addresses the question, 'what are changelings?' Locke's suggestion that they are something between man and beast would be rejected by those who work with specific real essences, the assumption being that no other species can come between man and beast (4.4.13). He insists that "the *Idea* of the Shape, Motion, and Life of a Man without Reason, is as much a distinct *Idea*, and makes as much a distinct *sort* of Things from Man and Beast, as the *Idea* of the Shape of an *Ass* with Reason, would be different from either that of Man or Beast, and be a Species of an Animal between, or distinct from both". To the question of what happens to such creatures as changelings when they die, he replies that that will be up to God. "They are in the hands of a faithful Creator and a bountiful Father, who disposes not of his Creatures according to our narrow Thoughts or Opinions, nor distinguishes them according to Names and Species of our Contrivance" (4.4.14). He then adds a feature of the transition from this life to the next: "And we that know so little of this present World we are in, may, I think, content our selves without being peremptory in defining the different states, which Creatures shall come into, when they go off this Stage". 'Different states' in this passage, it was 'gentle degrees' in 3.6.12.[3]

So far I have traced the use of the term 'creature' in several of Locke's books. It is also a term found rather extensively in *Two Treatises*, both the First and Second Treatise.[4] The occurrences of that term in his critique of Filmer follow Filmer's use of it, although Locke tends to add phrases to the term that Filmer does not use. Filmer will write 'creatures' or 'living creatures', and in his commentary Locke will write 'inferior or irrational Creatures' (§23), or he paraphrases Filmer by writing 'ranks of terrestrial Creatures' (§25), or 'terrestrial irrational Creatures' (§27). Other references in both his quotations from Filmer and in his commentary include: 'species of creatures' (§§28, 30), 'intellectual creatures' (§30).

These terms and phrases appear in almost every section of the First Treatise. Of course, the term has a biblical and Christian heritage, so it is not surprising to find the language of creatures (and their Creator) in the discussion of Filmer, but Locke continues to use the term in many sections of the Second Treatise, his political essay. Here too he refers to man and animals, no creatures above man. Some of the references to rational creatures give us a bit of information about such creatures in society. For example, if a Monarch invades a man's property, the man "has not only no Appeal, as those in Society ought to have, but [it] is as if he were degraded from the common state of Rational Creatures", since he is "denied a liberty to judge of, or to defend his Right" (§91). Explaining his principle that the "consent of the majority" should be taken as "the act of the whole", Locke contrasts this with the notion that only the consent of every individual in the society would be the act of the whole. This notion would only result in the dissolution of the society because it is unworkable. To require the consent of every individual would mean that rational creatures "should desire and constitute Societies only to be dissolved" (§98). Section 124 says that "the Law of Nature" is "plain and intelligible to all rational Creatures", even though they may be "biassed by their interests, as well as ignorant [of the law] from want of study of it". A society of rational creatures is characterized as one where individuals join "for their mutual good" and place "Rulers over themselves, to guard, and promote their good" (§163).

1.2. Beings

Locke's frequent use of the term 'beings', a kind of neutral, secular word, is of some significance if we want to understand what we might call 'Locke's universe'. The universe is populated with a variety of kinds of Beings; different labels are used to describe members of the universe. We can divide the Beings into three groups: (1) a material, corporeal group, (2) an intelligent, thinking group, and (3) a spiritual group. The latter consists of Beings above man on the scale of being. The members of the first two groups are finite and created; some, perhaps all (Locke is not clear about this) of those in the third group are also created.

He refers to the members of the first group in various ways: substantial, solid, corporeal, inanimate, material, insensitive, incogitative. These Beings appear in some of Locke's explications of particular claims or notions. For example, in explicating his concept of space without body, he offers the thought experiment of God placing "a Man at the extremity of corporeal Beings", where the man would be able to "stick his Hand beyond his Body" (2.13.21). Similarly for duration: we are able (Locke speaks of the mind being able) to enlarge the ideas of duration without limit, at least "beyond the existence of all corporeal Beings . . . of the World" (2.15.3). Section 6 of this same chapter refers to "the particular Extension and Place, of

The World of God, Angels, and Spirits 69

all corporeal Beings". *Essay* 4.3.24 comments on our ignorance of "the whole stupendious frame of Corporeal Beings", and 4.4.15 refers to the "Soul or Spirit, upon whose account alone some corporeal Beings have hitherto been concluded immortal". That same section speaks of material Beings, as also does 4.3.27 and 4.16.12. Another label for the Beings in this group is 'substantial' (4.12.9; 4.8.9; 4.3.28; 3.6.14). This label occurs in his discussion of the traditional notion of substance. Still other labels are 'solid' as in "solid Beings, which could not think", in contrast with "thinking Beings that are not extended" (2.13.16); inanimate and insensible Beings that we love and hate (2.20.5),[5] and incogitative Beings (4.10.9).

The labels for the Beings in the second group are: intelligent, intellectual, cogitative, thinking, knowing, sensible, and moral. Some of these characteristics are shared with members of the third group. The long chapter on power refers to the liberty of intellectual Beings, their ability to suspend judgment and deliberate about actions to be performed. This is, Locke says, the "great privilege of finite intellectual Beings", Beings such as ourselves (2.21.52). The archetypes for names and ideas in the minds of intelligent Beings are discussed in 3.6.43, in which he talks about the names for substances. In the famous section on thinking matter, men are referred to as "sensible intelligent Beings" (4.3.6). In 4.3.23, man is described as "the lowest of intellectual Beings". In section 27 of this chapter he refers to the minds of thinking Beings in other men as well as in ourselves (see also 2.13.16). *Essay* 4.10.9 gives a broad classification of "two sorts of Beings in the World, that Man knows, or conceives". It would be helpful were we able to find some clarification of this dual process of knowing and conceiving. Locke does not seem to analyze the act of conceiving, although he refers to what can and cannot be conceived throughout the *Essay*.[6] The two sorts of beings in this passage are material beings "without Sense, Perception, or Thought" and "Sensible, thinking, perceiving Beings, such as we find our selves to be" (for 'sensible', see also 1.1.1).[7] This classification is the same as that of incogitative and cogitative. Section 16 of this chapter refers to some men (unnamed) who think of themselves as "material thinking Beings". There Locke was writing against those who would make God material. He makes the case in several previous sections that matter cannot think. He had, of course, already suggested that God could add thought to a system of organized matter (4.3.6), but he wants to make the point here that matter does not in fact think and cannot do so without God's intervention. He obviously is arguing in section 16 against some unnamed materialists, men who, on Locke's account, took themselves to be examples of thinking matter.[8] Two other labels for the members of the second group are worth mention, moral Beings (3.5.12) and knowing Beings (4.10.12). For Locke the former of these was of great importance.

The first group of Beings in Locke's world are the material, physical objects, the objects and processes studied by experimental science. The second group gives us the characteristics of humans. Locke's *Essay* is an examination of the extent and nature of our knowledge of that physical world, the part that is available to us. His recommended method was that of experience and observation. When we come to sketch the characteristics of the Beings in the third group, he does not give much attention to how we know about the members of this group. Some readers may not give much importance to his rather detailed and extensive account of the Beings above us on the scale or chain of being. But it is clear that for Locke this group was a significant feature of the universe.

1.3. Spirits and Angels

As early as 1.4.9, he argues against the innatists that, were the idea of God found in every nation (which he thinks is not the case), that would not prove that idea to be innate. No more would the lack of the idea be an argument against God's existence. Similarly, if we have no distinct ideas of "various species of Angels, or intelligent Beings above us", that would not be an argument against the existence of such Beings. Another term for spirits may be 'pure intelligencies', a term used by Malebranche who distinguished four ways of knowing, the fourth being 'conjecture', which is how we know (an odd sense of 'know') "the Souls of other Men, and pure Intelligencies".[9] In his commentary on Malebranche in his Examination, Locke does not mention his own use of conjecture, nor does he distinguish conjecture from knowledge except to say, "We know them [pure intelligencies] not at all; but we probably think there are such Beings really existing in *rerum natura*". Perhaps 'think' plays the role of conjecture in this comment. Locke suggests that Malebranche should be talking about the ideas we have of souls and intelligencies, not whether such really exist. He continues his commentary: "For when he says, we know not Angels, either *in themselves*, or *by their Ideas*, or by *Consciousness*, what in that place does *Angel* signifie? What Idea in him does it stand for?" In section §53, he calls attention to Malebranche's talk "of *universal Reason* which *enlightens* every one, *whereof all Men* partake". Locke remarks: this "seems to me nothing else but the Power Men have to consider the Ideas they have one with another, and by thus comparing them, find out the relations that are between them". He then gives an example: "if an intelligent Being at one end of the World, and another at the other end of the World, will consider twice two and four together, he cannot but find them to be equal, i.e. to be the same Number" (pp. 205–6).

A passage in *Essay* 2.2.3 raises the possibility of other intelligent Beings with faculties more perfect than ours. Locke's analysis of memory finds him making a similar suggestion: "superiour created intellectual Beings" whose faculties far exceed our faculties (2.10.9). Here the suggestion is that the faculties of these Beings would be such that they may "have constantly in view the whole Scene of all their former actions, wherein no one of the thoughts they have ever had, may slip out of their sight".[10] It is "glorious Spirits" who are the topic here, God's "immediate Attendants". Not just past actions, but all past knowledge is available to these Beings. There are several degrees of such Angels, they may probably "have larger views, and some of them be endowed with capacities able to retain together, and constantly set before them, as in one Picture, all their past knowledge at once".[11] These are some of the ways we may suppose "wherein the knowledge of separate Spirits may exceedingly surpass ours" (2.10.9; see also 2.1.15).

Another reference to the abilities of angels and spirits occurs in the "Conduct". "Here we may imagine a vast and almost infinite Advantage that Angels and separate Spirits may have over us; who in their several degrees of Elevation above us, may be endowed with more comprehensive Faculties, and some of them perhaps have perfect and exact Views of all finite Beings that come under their Consideration, can, as it were, in the twinkling of an Eye, collect together all their scatter'd and almost boundless Relations" (§2, p. 9). See also his "A Discourse of Miracles": "We know good and bad Angels have Abilities and Excellencies exceedingly beyond all our poor Performances or narrow Comprehensions" (p. 231). With this ascription of special abilities to angels and other spirits, Locke goes on to say that we are unable to know "what is the utmost extent of Power that any of them has".[12]

It is some indication of the ease with which Locke refers to angels that they appear in the discussion of topics unrelated to such Beings. The remark I cited earlier from 2.10.9, about the ability of spirits to hold in one view all their past knowledge, is in the chapter on retention, memory. The chapter on duration uses angels as an explication of some feature of time. For example, 2.15.7 makes the point that time is applied to parts of what Locke calls "infinite Duration". Such talk of parts of time can be misleading if we assume that there really are parts of time to be "really distinguished and measured out by this real Existence, and periodical Motions of Bodies that were appointed from the Beginning to be for Signs, and for Seasons, and for Days, and Years". We may suppose that some parts of "infinite uniform Duration" are "equal to certain lengths of measured Time; and so consider them as bounded and determined". Then he illustrates this point: "For if we should suppose the Creation, or Fall of the Angels, was at the Beginning of the *Julian* Period, we should speak properly enough, and should be understood, if we said, 'tis a longer time since the Creation of Angels, than the Creation of the World, by 764 years". In that way we would in effect "mark out so much of that undistinguished Duration, as we suppose equal to, and would have admitted, 764 annual Revolutions of the Sun, moving at the rate it now does". Later in this same chapter, where he makes some comparisons between duration and expansion, one difference is that duration "is one common measure of all Existence whatsoever, wherein all things whilst they exist, equally partake. For this present moment is common to all things, that are now in being, and equally comprehends that part of their Existence, as much as if they were all but one single Being" (2.15.11). Then he raises the possibility that angels and spirits may have something similar with respect to expansion, expansion being space without body, although he says that possibility is "beyond my Comprehension".[13] Another chapter, this one on number, uses a brief reference to angels. Number is "the most universal *Idea* we have"; it "applies it self to Men, Angels, Actions, Thoughts, every thing that either doth exist, or can be imagined" (2.16.1).

The existence of angels was not imagined or even supposed: Locke seems simply to accept (believe in) their existence. Supposition enters when he attempts to suggest some specific feature or ability that angels or spirits may have. *Essay* 2.21.49 goes beyond the probable and supposition: "If we look upon those *superiour Beings* above us, who enjoy perfect Happiness, we shall have reason to judge that they are more steadily *determined in their choice of Good* than we; and yet we have no reason to think they are less happy, or less free, than we are". A passage in book 4 seems to limit happiness to "superior Ranks of Spirits", perhaps meaning that inferior ranks are not happy, or happy to a lesser degree (4.3.6). Section 36 of 2.23 simply asserts: "we must necessarily conclude, that separate Spirits, which are Beings that have perfecter Knowledge, and greater Happiness than we, must needs have also a perfecter way of communicating their Thoughts, than we have".[14]

2. Locke's Extravagant Conjecture

There is one other passage concerning the abilities of angels and spirits that merits attention. Locke offers what he labels "an extravagant Conjecture" or 'wild fancy': that spirits can "assume to themselves Bodies of different Bulk, Figure, and Conformation of Parts" (2.23.13). The conjecture does not apply to the existence of spirits, only to the possibility of their assuming different bodily forms and with different, more forceful sense organs. Such spirits would be able to see the corpuscular structure of bodies. The previous section had raised that possibility for us, the microscopical eye passage. Locke concluded there that heightened sense organs of this magnitude would be a handicap for us in our world, not an asset. He thinks altered sense organs would not be a disadvantage for spirits; such abilities would be one "great advantage some of them have over us", the ability to "so frame, and shape to themselves Organs of Sensation or Perception, as to suit them to their present Design, and the Circumstances of the Object they would consider" (2.23.13). Just think, he muses, how much a man would "exceed all others in Knowledge, who had but the Faculty so to alter the Structure of his Eyes, that one Sense, as to make it capable of all the several degrees of Vision, which the assistance of Glasses (casually at first light on) has taught us to conceive?" Such an alteration would enable us to see the particles of blood or even the structure of the matter of bodies. But, as he remarked here and in the previous section, such an increase in our vision would only hinder us in our world.

These two sections (2.23.12 and 13) make for intriguing reading. They read as if Locke was torn between two powerful notions, one sober, the other fanciful but attractive, even alluring. The sober notion is that God has given us all the faculties we need for this life, and these are no mean faculties. "We are able, by our Senses, to know, and distinguish things; and to examine them so far, as to apply them to our Uses, and several ways to accommodate the Exigencies of this Life. We have insight enough into their admirable Contrivances, and wonderful Effects, to admire, and magnify the Wisdom, Power, and Goodness of their Author" (2.23.12). God did not intend for us to "have a perfect, clear, and adequate Knowledge" of the material world. The knowledge we have is sufficient to lead us to admire and magnify God, as well as to lead us to the knowledge of the creatures in the world and thence to a knowledge of God. These religious values go along with practical knowledge for life, "for the Conveniences of living". To wish for an increase in the power of our sense organs, as with the spirits in his extravagant conjecture, would almost be an affront to God.

But for Locke, the second, fanciful notion apparently had its strong attraction. In the several examples in section 12, we hear echoes of that a priori, deductive science of nature which he detailed but denied to man. He dwells on the possibilities before dismissing them as impractical. Here are some of his musings and reflections on the possibilities and the knowledge they would provide. In each case, the conjectures are followed by a warning, showing how they would not after all be useful.

(1) Were "our Senses alter'd, and made much quicker and acuter, the appearance and outward Scheme of things would have quite another Face to us" (p. 302, lines 26–28). But he quickly adds, such a condition "would be inconsistent with our Being, or at least [our] well-being in this part of the Universe".

(2) "If our Sense of Hearing were but 1000 times quicker than it is", we might think it an advantage, but a perpetual noise [which we would experience] would distract us, and in the "quietest Retirement, [we would] be less able to sleep or meditate, than in the middle of a Sea-fight" (pp. 302–3).

(3) Calling vision (seeing) "the most instructive of our Senses", he remarks: "were [it] in any Man 1000, or 100000 times more acute than it is now by the best Microscope, things several millions of times less than the smallest Object of his sight now, would then be visible to his naked

Eyes, and so he would come nearer the Discovery of the Texture and Motion of the minute Parts of corporeal things; and in many of them, probably get *Ideas* of their internal Constitutions" (p. 303). The attraction of such a possibility is quickly put down by the remark that we would then be "in a quite different World from other People", discourse about objects would be impossible, and we could not talk about the colors of objects. Moreover, we would not be able to endure bright light.

(4) With enhanced vision, microscopical eyes, "a Man could penetrate farther than ordinary into the secret Composition, and radical Texture of Bodies", but such enhanced vision would not be of use in the market or at the Exchange.

(5) Anyone that "was sharp-sighted enough to see the Configuration of the minute Particles of the Spring of a Clock, and observe upon what peculiar Structure and Impulse its elastick Motion depends, would no doubt discover something very admirable", but such a man would not be able to see the hands of the clock or "the Characters of the Hour-plate, and thereby at a distance see what a-Clock it was". With such vision, we would gain the discovery of "the secret Contrivance of the Parts of the Machin", but we would lose the use of the clock.

These examples may be seen as a partial application of that extravagant conjecture to humans, but the knowledge gained would be useless, no matter how insightful and how much our knowledge would be enlarged. The case of angels and spirits is different, perhaps because Locke depicts them as mainly concerned with knowledge, not action. They do not act in the market-place or the Exchange. At least in this conjecture, knowledge alone is what they would acquire.

Why Locke introduces this conjecture at all is not clear. Its function in this section may be, in part, to serve as an example of altered sense-organs (in this case, the eyes) for some Beings who unlike humans, could benefit from such sense organs. Taking on bodily form means that these spirits inhabit those bodies. Do those bodies differ from human bodies, would their physiology of vision be different from our physiology? One difference is that their bodies have adjustable sense organs, at least adjustable eyes. But besides being a fascinating suggestion, what is the purpose of Locke's wild fancy? Does he mean that assuming bodily form with special sense organs is necessary for spirits to penetrate the structure of bodies? Are the superior faculties spirits have not able to give them a knowledge of the inner constitution of physical objects without assuming bodily form? Locke does not specify the particular nature of the faculties and abilities of angels and spirits, but I assume those faculties do not require a physical body. So the reason for Locke's extravagant conjecture remains unclear. Perhaps this conjecture is designed to provide an empirical basis for the knowledge spirits have of the structure of matter, a knowledge derived from sense experience. The passage in 4.3.6 about superior ranks of spirits credits them with "quicker and more penetrating Sight" than we have, but he does not link this remark with the extravagant conjecture. When it comes to communicating their thoughts, Locke does not believe they need bodies, so whether they can see or know the structure of matter without bodies or superior sense organs is left undetermined.[15]

3. Two Properties of That World

3.1. Perfection

The concept of perfection is somewhat vague in Locke's account. There are only a few examples of specific perfections. A perfect language is one where the word-signs "can be made use of, as *to comprehend several particular Things*" (3.1.3). The chapter on the imperfection of words refers to the imperfection of language and of words, making it difficult to know their signification (3.9.1). Another example of perfection is in complex ideas of modes, especially mixed modes. They are perfect because the ideas have all the content intended, the fit between ideas and their referents is perfect (2.31.3). He contrasts these ideas with the imperfection of ideas of substances where the fit between ideas and objects is only partial at best; the ideas do not capture the inner constitution of substances on which all their properties depend. Late in the *Essay,* Locke mentions the highest perfection of reason: in finding proofs and making discoveries (4.17.6). Remarking that our knowledge is "limited to our *Ideas*", he says our knowledge "cannot exceed them either in extent, or perfection", suggesting perhaps that there are degrees of perfection within human experience (4.3.6; cf. 3.11.22). He continues in this section to refer to "humane Perfection" without clarifying what that perfection is. He recognizes the limits of our knowledge, especially in relation to what he refers to as "Allbeing', but he stresses that there is still room for improvement and extension of our knowledge beyond where it is now.

I think we can find some hints at human perfection by looking at some particular features or aspects of man. He refers to the perfection and order of a rational being while contrasting that order with the disorganized and incoherent thoughts we have sometimes while dreaming (2.1.6). Another passage speaks of "every part and organ in perfection" working in accord with God's design (2.7.4). Still another example of human perfection may be virtue, at least that is what "one of the *Heathen* Philosophers" would say (1.3.5). Locke might agree: virtue is high on his list of educational goals. He characterized virtue in the *Reasonableness* as perfection.[16] Two other passages relating to human perfection concern action, or at least some of the preludes to action. It is not, he says in *Essay* 2.21.47, "a fault, but a perfection of our nature to desire, will, and act according to the last result of a fair *Examination*". Section 48 of that chapter identifies another perfection: when desire and preferring are determined by good. Moreover, "the certainer such determination is, the greater is the perfection". Locke also writes about the ideas of existence, knowledge, power, pleasure, and happiness, saying that "the more we have of each, the better" (3.6.11). He must mean not the ideas, but the referents of those ideas. He does not speak of perfection in this passage, but the implication seems to be there. He does not explain what having more existence would be for us or for other spirits.

3.3.1. Happiness: The Happy God. The notion of having more happiness, or of one person being happier than another, or of a person being happier at one time than at another does have some recognizable plausibility. When we are required to apply happiness to angels and other spirits in their intellectual world, we may find some difficulty in understanding what happiness is for those Beings. Locke admits in an early Journal entry that "our idea of happiness, such as the blessed enjoy and such as we are capable of, is very imperfect in this World".[17] The difficulty increases when we try to understand the happiness of God: "God Almighty himself is under the necessity of being happy" (2.21.50).

This startling statement about the happy God was no passing fancy or whimsy on Locke's part. The ascription of happiness to God is repeated in four other, later passages. It comes up twice in his discussion of our ideas of substance. (1) The ideas we have "both of God, and separate Spirits, are made up of the simple *Ideas* we receive from *Reflection*" (2.23.33). The ideas he cites there are existence, duration, knowledge, power, and happiness, and "several other [unnamed] Qualities and Powers, which it is better to have, than to be without". He then says we enlarge or join each of these ideas with the idea of infinity, thereby we have "our complex *Idea of God*". (2) In section 35 of this chapter, Locke is quick to point out that of course we do not know God's essence, no more than we know the real essence of "a Peble, or a Fly, or of our own selves". He is confident enough to say God is "simple and uncompounded", but our idea of him is composed of a number of other ideas. His list in the first sentence of that section is existence, power, and knowledge, with an 'etc.' tacked on at the end. The final long sentence of that section adds happiness. "I think, I may say we have no other *Idea* of him, but a complex one of Existence, Knowledge, Power, Happiness, *etc.* infinite and eternal". Together, these make up "the *Idea* or Notion we have of God". (3) Section 36 says that "there is no *Idea* we attribute to God, bating Infinity, which is not also a part of our complex *Idea* of other Spirits", the list here being "Knowledge, Power, Duration, Happiness, *etc.*". (4) A similar list to those in 2.23.35 and 36, with pleasure added, is given in the chapter on the names of substances.

> Thus having got from reflecting on our selves, the *Idea* of Existence, Knowledge, Power, and Pleasure, each of which we find it better to have than to want; and the more we have of each, the better; joyning all these together, with infinity to each of them, we have the complex *Idea* of an eternal, omniscient, omnipotent, infinitely wise, and happy Being. (3.6.11)

Pleasure may be on the list because of Locke's general association of happiness with pleasure, intellectual pleasure, I assume, in God's case.[18]

These three ascriptions of happiness to God may just be a report on the idea of God that Locke's man forms. At least, I do not think Locke was suggesting that all men, all humans, form the idea of God in this way. There may be a prescriptive aspect to Locke's account. Just why he selects the ideas he does, rather than others that we also have, is not clear, although with the exception of pleasure and happiness, the properties in his lists are some of the standard ones in Christian theology. What stands out, what seems both novel and surprising, is the inclusion of happiness among these properties. Even so, it is one thing to say God enjoys perfect, complete happiness, along with eternal duration and great power and knowledge. It is something else to say, as Locke says in the 2.21.50 passage, that God is under the necessity to be happy. What kind of necessity is this—logical, metaphysical? Does God have of necessity all the properties on Locke's lists? Given the nature of an infinite Being, that Being must exist, God cannot not exist? This was one way of viewing God's existence. I suppose Locke would say all the properties of God flow from his nature, his nature determines them all, and of necessity all follow from God's nature. He does say in the chapter on the knowledge of the existence of God, that "from the Consideration of our selves, and what we infallibly find in our own Constitutions, our Reason leads us to the Knowledge of this certain and evident Truth, That *there is an eternal, most powerful, and most knowing Being*" (4.10.6). He then says that from this idea when "duly considered, will easily be deduced all those other Attributes, which we ought to ascribe to this eternal Being". He does not say what additional attributes could be deduced. It makes sense to say the attributes of God may follow from his nature, but we do not have a knowledge of his nature, essence, or inner constitution. The deduction Locke claims could be made is not from God's nature, but only from the idea of an eternal powerful and knowing Being. How such a deduction could include the property of being happy is not at all clear. Locke seems to be making both an epistemic claim (we could deduce the properties of God from our idea of God) and an ontic claim (some or all of God's properties flow from his nature or essence). In the absence of a knowledge of his nature, we can form an idea of some of his attributes and deduce others from that idea. At the very least, the assertion that God is "under the necessity of being happy" sounds like a categorical assertion about one of the properties or features of God. The discussion in the sections preceding section 50 is designed to meet an objection to Locke's claim that "every Man is put under a necessity by his constitution, as an intelligent Being, to be determined in *willing* by his own Thought and Judgment, what is best for him to do: else he would be under the determination of some other than himself, which is want of Liberty" (2.21.48). He wants to make the point that this sort of necessity and being determined does not conflict with liberty, it is in fact true liberty. "The constant desire of Happiness, and the constraint it puts upon us to act for it, no Body, I think, accounts an abridgment of *Liberty*, or at least an abridgment of *Liberty* to be complain'd of" (2.21.50). In the same way, God is determined by his nature to be happy.

There is a problem when we try to understand (form an idea of) the happiness of a happy God, of the happiness of those superior ranks of spirits, and even the promised lasting, durable happiness awaiting just men. The problem consists in not knowing what happiness is when applied to the Beings in the intellectual world, especially when applied to God. It is not even easy to find a clear definition of happiness in this life in Locke's extended discussion in chapter 21. It is associated with pleasure. He does distinguish intellectual from physical pleasure but there is no clear account of intellectual pleasure. There is an entry in his Journal for 16 July 1676 which shows his awareness of the difficulty of conceiving of happiness when extended to other spirits and to the next life. Our "idea of happiness, such as the blessed enjoy and such as we are capable of, is very imperfect in this world". This remark was preceded by referring to "the pleasures of spiritual objects (which certainly as more proportioned to the nature of the mind are more capable to touch and move it with lovely and ravishing delights) to us who, being immersed in the body and beset with material objects, when they are continually importuning us, have very little sense or perception of spiritual things, which are as it were at a distance and affect us but seldom".[19] Perhaps the happiness of spirits (and God) is just their superior knowledge.

3.3.2. Happiness: The Chief End of Man.

References to happiness pervade the *Essay*. A case could almost be made for saying Locke was obsessed with happiness. The long chapter on power (2.21) is filled with references to happiness (30 of the 73 sections give happiness a prominent place in the discussion); chapter 27 contains a few references of importance for personal identity (the concern for happiness); and there are scattered comments on happiness in other chapters. The last two chapters give happiness, especially eternal happiness, a prominent place in the discussion. Locke announces early on that nature "has put into Man a desire of Happiness, and an aversion to Misery" (1.3.3). Desire and aversion are even described as innate principles. Other passages express this basic drive for happiness and aversion to misery in different ways. *Essay* 2.21.36 says that "the present *uneasiness*, that we are under, does naturally determine the will, in order to that happiness which we all aim at in our actions". Section 39 asserts that "we constantly desire happiness"; section 43 says "every one constantly pursues" happiness; section 47 speaks of our pursuit and endeavor for happiness; section 52 speaks of "the inclination, and tendency" of our nature to seek happiness; section 54 repeats the claim that "all Men desire Happiness"; section 55 says "all Men's desires tend to Happiness"; section 57 confirms again that all men "aim at being happy"; section 61 says all men "in earnest pursue Happiness"; section 62 tells us that "every intelligent Being [this includes Beings other than men] really seeks Happiness"; section 68 makes the ringing assertion, "all Men desire Happiness, that's past doubt", and happiness there is described as man's "great end" and goes on to refer to "this general Desire of Happiness"; section 71 says, "all that we desire is only to be Happy", and continues by remarking "this general *Desire* of Happiness operates constantly and invariably"; and 2.27.18 says that "Happiness and Misery" are what "every one is concerned for *himself*". *Essay* 2.21.51 describes the "unalterable pursuit of happiness in general", of "true and solid happiness" as "our greatest good".[20] The final chapter of the *Essay* singled out happiness as an end of action; ethics is described as "the seeking out those Rules, and Measures of humane Actions, which lead to Happiness" (4.21.3). The "Conduct" characterizes theology as, among other things, concerned with "the Honour and Veneration of the Creator, and the Happiness of Mankind" (§22, p. 66). The *Reasonableness* says mankind "must be allowed to pursue their Happiness", happiness being "their chief End" (p. 161). In that book, he also speaks of persuading men "that if they live well here, they shall be happy hereafter" (p. 163).

Happiness pops up in some of the discussions of seemingly unrelated topics—topics unrelated to happiness. While rejecting the claim of innatists that, because moral laws are broken does not mean the law is not innate, Locke paints a picture of a society of men void of humanity and confounding "the known and natural measures of Right and Wrong". Such a society would be "look'd on, as the professed Enemy of their Peace and Happiness" (1.3.11). In his rejection of the Cartesian claim that the soul always thinks, he asks: "If the *Soul* doth *think in a sleeping Man*, without being conscious of it, I ask, whether, during such thinking, it has any Pleasure or Pain, or be capable of Happiness or Misery?" (2.1.11). His answer is firm: "to be happy or miserable without being conscious of it, seems to me utterly inconsistent and impossible". If it be supposed that the soul can exist apart from the body while the man sleeps, and the soul thinks, feels pleasure and pain; the consequence would be two persons, e.g. Socrates asleep and Socrates awake. Socrates awake "has no Knowledge of, or Concernment for that Happiness, or Misery of his Soul". A similar point is made in the next section where happiness and misery play a role again. Explicating the utility of pain and pleasure as guides for what to avoid and what to seek, Locke suggests that one reason for God having mixed pleasure and pain in almost all our "Thoughts and Senses" is that, since we find "imperfection, dissatisfaction, and want of complete happiness, in all the Enjoyments which the Creatures can afford us, [we] might be led to seek it in the enjoyment of him [God]" (2.7.5). The chapter on pleasure and pain contrasts "our *Love* and *Hatred* of inanimate insensible Beings" with our love and hatred of "Beings capable of Happiness or Misery" (2.20.5). Love and hatred in this case "is often the Uneasiness or Delight, which we find in our selves arising from a consideration of their very Being, or Happiness".

Being capable of happiness or misery is one of the defining

features of Locke's person, as *Essay* 2.27.17, 18, 25, and 27 make clear. Happiness and misery come in varying degrees (see, for example, 2.21.63, 64). Above we saw a reference to 'complete' happiness. The greatest degree comes to some in the next life; there are infinite degrees, in fact (2.21.44 and 2.21.50). A Christian "has the view of Happiness and Misery in another Life" (1.3.5).[21] Divine "Justice shall bring to Judgment, at the last Day, the very same Persons, to be happy or miserable in the other, who did well or ill in this Life" (1.4.5). He describes happiness in the next life as 'perfect' for a Christian "who hath a prospect of the different State of perfect Happiness or Misery, that attends all Men after this Life, depending on their Behaviour here" (2.21.60). There are several references in the *Reasonableness* to "that Happy state of Immortality" (pp. 12, 104). Earlier in that work, Locke explained that Jesus' disciples spoke of the Kingdom of God (the second intellectual world) as "*the World to come,* which they believed was to put an end to *this World*: And that then the Just should be raised from the Dead; to enjoy, in that *new World,* a Happy Eternity" (pp. 94–95). He describes such happiness in the *Essay* as 'endless' or 'durable'; the misery is characterized as 'exquisite'. An earlier section speaks of "a perfect, secure, and lasting happiness in a future State" (2.21.44). Locke says these states apply to "the immortal Soul hereafter". Some passages speak of 'felicity' or 'bliss' (2.21.50, 60), and 2.21.44 refers to "a state of eternal durable Joys after this life", and "the joys of Heaven"; they surpass "all the good is to be had here".[22]

Section 3 of chapter 20, book 4, the penultimate chapter, comes back to the Christian theme of happiness in the next life. Voicing concern that "the greatest part of Mankind, by the necessity of their Condition, subjected to unavoidable Ignorance in those Things, which are of greatest Importance to them", he raises what I suspect is a rhetorical question: "Have the Bulk of Mankind no other Guide, but Accident, and blind Chance, to conduct them to their Happiness, or Misery?" He speaks of our greatest concernment as being for our "everlasting Happiness, or Misery". His opinion is clear: "No Man is so wholly taken up with the Attendance on the Means of Living, as to have no spare Time at all to think of his Soul, and inform himself in Matters of Religion". Locke had earlier identified "Virtue and Religion" as necessary for happiness (2.21.60).

Conclusion

The second intellectual world of God, Angels and Spirits, and the world to come for just men, contains a variety of Beings, their numbers unspecified, differing among them in ways that constitute species marked by degrees of perfection in knowledge and happiness. A few of the Beings have a special status as God's immediate attendants. These special Beings (he characterized them as 'glorious spirits') are angels, Beings that the *OED* explains are "a ministering spirit or divine messenger; one of an order of spiritual beings superior to man in power and intelligence, who are the attendants and messengers of the Deity". The language is exactly that employed by Locke. He named two standard biblical types, Cherubims and Seraphims (4.3.17). In what ways, other than their function as messengers and attendants on the Deity, these spirits differ from other spirits, he does not say. They are both 'species' of spirits. What he says about non-angelic spirits conforms to the *OED* definitions of 'spirit': "Incorporeal or immaterial being, as opposed to body or matter; being or intelligence conceived as distinct from, or independent of anything physical or material". Part of a second definition also fits Locke's account, except for the last word: "a supernatural, incorporeal, rational being, or personality". Locke does not speak of the personality of spirits but he does use that term when writing about persons. The entry for 'personality' in the *OED* is again instructive. The first listed definition is: "The quality or fact of being a person; that quality which makes a being personal". The dictionary gives a 1678 usage, "a personal being, a person". A citation is also given from Paley: "These capacities constitute personality, for they imply consciousness and thought". Locke's forensic definition of 'person' that I discussed in chapter 1 said that "personality extends it self beyond present Existence, to what is past". It does so "only by consciousness, whereby it becomes concerned and accountable, owns and imputes to it *self* past Actions, just upon the same ground, and for the same reason, that it does the present" (2.27.26). It is odd to speak of personality, rather than the person, extending it self, but that term plays the role of person, or it designates the personhood, the personality of the self or the man. The property of being a person is extended by consciousness to past actions, in just the same way that it claims and appropriates present actions; consciousness, not memory, a point worth stressing.

The other occurrence of the term 'personality' is in section 22 of that same chapter, where the case of the man who does not remember what he did while drunk is discussed. The question was, do we hold him responsible for actions he does not remember doing? Locke explains that "though punishment be annexed to personality, and personality to consciousness", human courts "justly punish him; because the Fact is proved against him, but want of consciousness cannot be proved for him".[23] This example makes the same point about consciousness, not memory, appropriating actions. Memory is not a necessary condition for personal identity. The assumption in this example may be that since the fact of the man performing that action is established by witnesses, it must have been a conscious act at the time, at least, in the eyes of the law. Not only is it the case that consciousness appropriates actions, any actions I do are done consciously.

Keeping in mind Locke's use of 'personality', and with that term being part of one of the *OED* definitions of 'spirit', it is tempting to suggest that Locke might apply his analysis of personal identity to spirits. Not only are spirits intelligent beings, perhaps they qualify for Locke's account of persons and the actions they do. What the actions of the Beings are in the second intellectual world is left unspecified, except for the angels. These Beings all have faculties, some of which are similar to our faculties but more perfect; i.e. affording them knowledge without bodies, sense organs, brains or nerves. Towards what precisely such cognitive abilities are directed, Locke does not indicate. Whether that knowledge had by these immaterial spirits differs from those embodied spirits in Locke's extravagant conjecture, we cannot say. Perhaps the point of that conjecture was to construct an ideal human, an ideal cognitive human, perhaps even as an illustration or example of the constitution of man in the next life, where men will have some bodily form. We will see in the next chapter that man, a just man, will enter the second intellectual world, will join the spirits there. Again, the details are vague about the exact status of man in that world. Part of the answer depends on the status of man's soul in that world. We will need to ask whether the term 'personality', or indeed, 'intelligent Being', can in any way be applied to the soul that becomes a spirit and ascends the chain of being. I will explore these questions in chapter 5.

The three terms explored in this chapter, 'creatures', 'beings', and 'spirits' (and angels), do not refer to mutually discrete entities. At least, 'creatures' applies to animals, plants, man, and some Beings that ascend the scale of being towards infinite perfection and happiness. 'Creature' may not apply to angels, or to all spirits. But 'beings' seems to apply to everything on the chain except inanimate, insensible members of the universe. Or it may be that 'beings' applies to everything—it may be the most general term. Even God is a being, and as we will see, the spirits that inhabit our bodies are real Beings. The term 'spirit' is the least extensive term, applying only to the Beings in the domain of God, Angels and Spirits, and also to the souls that inhabit our bodies. Man, person, and agents are not spirits, although the person appears at the resurrection, presumably along with the man. If the term 'creature' means anything created by God, then it would also have wide application.

Intelligent Beings constitute a more restricted group. They seem to populate many mansions of the universe, even other planets and, of course, in the second intellectual world. It is tempting to say that world contains only intelligent Beings, even though some have (just men) bodies of some kind. The move up the chain is a move from materiality to immateriality. The soul as a real Being detaches itself from the human body at death and goes up the chain alone. I guess man does not move up the chain; humans bypass the chain and appear at the resurrection in the domain of God, Angels and Spirits. So is it the case that only immaterial Beings go up the chain? At the resurrection, do man and person join the soul?

These last few questions and remarks anticipate the analysis of the next two chapters, but it is salutary to raise them here.

CHAPTER FOUR

SPIRITS AND OUR IDEAS OF THEM

We have seen that the domain of God, Angels and Spirits is heavily populated with creatures, Beings and separate spirits. We are told that there are species of these, indicating that there are some differences among the different species or different kinds of those Beings. We are also told that there are ranks of these Beings, a reference I assume to an ordering, to different locations on the chain, different states, different degrees of being, different degrees of perfection and happiness. Locke's account of the chain of being in *Essay* 3.6.12, 22, and 23 does not offer many details on the creatures above man. The examples illustrating the gradations between creatures below man are of animals. He mentions fish, birds, porpoises, mules, apes, elephants, along with vegetables and plants. Intelligent creatures are only briefly mentioned. Nevertheless, it is clear that the intellectual world of angels and spirits, a world that he describes as 'beautiful', fascinated and held great importance for him. That world was, after all, the hoped-for destination of virtuous and just men.

Three topics remain to be explored: (1) how do we form ideas of spirits, (2) what information do we have about them, or, if 'information' is the wrong word, on what do we base our ideas of them, and (3) what is the place and role of man's soul in this life and in the next?

1. Ideas of Spirits

In his *Essays on the Law of Nature*, Locke listed understanding, reason, and sense perception as three ways of knowing.[1] These ways of knowing can, "by the help of nature and his [a man's] own sagacity", enable us to enquire "into the nature and functions of spirits and minds and the laws that apply to them" (p. 125).[2] He may be using the term 'spirit' in a different way here from the sense discussed so far (spirit as intelligent Beings above us), since the claim of knowing the nature of spirits is too ambitious, given Locke's later skepticism about going beyond experienced qualities. He might be thought to be using the term 'spirit' as he does 'mind', but in this passage he does seem to distinguish spirit from mind. So I think we can safely say this early writing refers to Beings above us on the chain of being. What the laws would be that apply to spirits, or even to minds, he does not say. If he means the law of nature, the term 'mind' must stand for man or person, since it is for these that the law was prescribed. The confident claim that enquiry can be or has been made into the nature and function of minds was in fact fulfilled in his *Essay*. But to make the same claim about our knowledge of spirits seems over confident if that is his claim. Nor is it at all clear how sense perception could lead us to any knowledge or even beliefs about spirits. If reason is the faculty that is the source of such knowledge, he does not indicate how that faculty could lead to that result. The faculty of understanding as the source is even more dubious.

Even if he was over-confident about what we can know about spirits, he does give some attention to how we form ideas of them: "For the Mind getting, only by reflecting on its own Operations, those simple *Ideas* which it attributes to *Spirits*, it hath, or can have no other Notion of *Spirit*, but by attributing all those Operations, it finds in it self, to a sort of Beings, without Consideration of Matter" (3.6.11).[3] Just as we form the idea of God by combining ideas of existence, knowledge, power, pleasure, happiness, with infinity added to each, so the idea of spirits contains all the same ideas, including happiness, with the idea of infinity deleted (2.23.36). He had earlier explained how we can form the idea of "all things existing" or that can possibly exist (2.23.34).

His explication of how such an all-encompassing idea is formed is rather curious. "If I find, that I know some few things, and some of them, or all, perhaps, imperfectly, I can frame an *Idea* of knowing twice as many; which I can double again, as often as I can add to Number, and thus enlarge my *Idea* of Knowledge, by extending its Comprehension to all things existing, or possible" (2.23.34). By 'enlarging his knowledge' he might be taken to mean the objects of knowledge. The text is not entirely clear. Does the enlargement enable him to comprehend, include, in the idea of knowledge all things existing or possible? We need to decide what it means to say of knowledge that it encompasses more and more things. Does it mean that we are able to apply certain other ideas to objects not available to experience? From 'all things existing or possible', in the next sentence he concludes: "The same also I can do of knowing them more perfectly". The word 'them' would seem to refer to any thing, any substance (the chapter is on the idea of substances). What 'the same' is must be enlarging and extending, but this enlarging is to "all their Qualities, Powers, Causes, Consequences, and Relations, *etc.*" of some substance. He adds: "till all be perfectly known, that is in them, or can any way relate to them". Now the word 'them' seems to refer to the qualities, powers, etc., or is it meant to refer to other features of the subject or substance? I think the reference is to both the substance and its qualities, powers, etc. The result is two-fold: (1) we would have that knowledge of things (substances, objects, bodies) without experience, the a priori science of nature that Locke detailed, were such a knowledge possible for us and (2) we would have the sort of knowledge that God, and perhaps some spirits have: an infinite, boundless knowledge of all things.

In summary, Locke's argument for forming the idea of such knowledge runs as follows. We ourselves know some things and we also discover that we can extend our knowledge beyond what it is at a particular time. We want to see whether we can have an idea (we might say, concept) of the knowledge that a superior Being may have. Such a Being would have a knowledge of all things existing or that could possibly exist. We start in this quest with the fact that in our little mansion of the universe we know some few things and we gradually increase our knowledge. We then form the idea of a knowledge which comprehends everything, 'allbeing', to use one of Locke's terms. There are limits to what we finite creatures can know; there are no limits for an infinite Being. So the process of enlarging applies to the idea of knowledge, the knowledge that an infinite Being would have. The process is repeated with other ideas in our experience, such as the idea of power enlarged to infinite power, or the idea of duration "without beginning or end".

1.1. The Operation of Enlarging Ideas

Locke explains that this process of enlarging works with the "simple *Ideas*, we have taken from the Operations of our own Minds" (2.23.34). Enlarging is one of the operations of the human mind. It comes under composition, "whereby it [the mind] puts together several of those simple ones it has received from Sensation and Reflection, and combines them into complex ones" (2.11.6). Enlarging is then explained: "though the Composition does not so much appear as in more complex ones, yet it is nevertheless a putting several *Ideas* together, though of the same kind". He gives an example: "Thus by adding several Unites together, we make the *Idea* of a dozen; and by putting together the repeated *Ideas* of several Perches, we frame that of Furlong".[4] Here and elsewhere the mind does the enlarging, but Locke does not, I think, mean that process is an automatic one done by the mind. We, not our minds, combine and repeat ideas and enlarge them in various ways. In some passages, it is thought that is enlarged. With children, such enlarging is a maturation process, part of learning as they experience more and more sensible objects (1.4.13). Children are also discussed in 3.3.7 in which Locke presents an account of general ideas:

"it will not perhaps be amiss, to trace our Notions, and Names, from their beginning, and observe by what degrees we proceed, and by what steps we enlarge our Ideas from our first Infancy". Another passage where thoughts are enlarged concerns Pascal's phenomenal memory: considering that great memory "may help us to enlarge our thoughts towards greater Perfections of it in superior ranks of Spirits" (2.10.9). Other passages suggest ways in which our knowledge, not our idea of knowledge, can be enlarged (4.5.10; 4.12.3, 14, 15; 4.17.4).

The process of enlarging that is most relevant to the formation of ideas of spirits (and of God) involves our ideas, as in the passage above from *Essay* 2.23.34. By examining other sections in which Locke uses examples of enlarging ideas, we may obtain a better understanding of the process and the result when we form ideas of spirits.

> 2.13.4 (Simple modes of space): "Men for the use, and by the custom of measuring, settle in their Minds the *Ideas* of certain stated lengths, such as are an *Inch, Foot, Yard, Fathom, Mile, Diameter of the Earth*, etc. which are so many distinct *Ideas* made up only of Space". These measures can then be repeated in their minds "as often as they will, without mixing or joining to them the *Idea* of Body, or any thing else; and frame to themselves the *Ideas* of long, square, or cubick, *Feet, Yards*, or *Fathoms*, here amongst the Bodies of the Universe, or else beyond the utmost Bounds of all Bodies; and by adding these still one to another, enlarge their *Idea* of Space as much as they please". That idea can be enlarged further without stopping and thereby reach the idea of immensity.

> 2.15.2 (Expansion): Having acquired "the *Idea* of the length of any part of *Expansion*", the mind can "repeat that *Idea*; and so adding it to the former, *enlarge its Idea of Length*, and make it equal to two Spans, or two Paces, and so as often as it will, till it equals the distance of any parts of the Earth one from another, and increase thus, till it amounts to the distance of the Sun, or remotest Star".

2.15.3 (Duration): "*The Mind having got the Idea of any length of Duration, can double, multiply, and enlarge it,* not only beyond its own, but beyond the existence of all corporeal Beings, and all the measures of Time, taken from the great Bodies of the World, and their Motions". He then adds a qualification: "But yet every one easily admits, That though we make Duration boundless, as certainly it is, we cannot yet extend it beyond all being". Locke then adds a comment about God: "GOD, every one easily allows, fills Eternity; and 'tis hard to find a Reason, why any one should doubt, that he likewise fills Immensity: His infinite Being is certainly as boundless one way as another; and methinks it ascribes a little too much to Matter, to say, where there is no Body, there is nothing". I suppose the qualification and limitation means that where there is no being at all, if such a state were possible, there would be no duration. Since God fills eternity and immensity, there is no part of the universe devoid of all being. Locke seems to have in mind two points: (1) the claim by some that "where there is no Body, there is nothing" and (2) the endorsement of the theological principle that God fills eternity and immensity.

These examples of enlarging ideas concern larger and more remote objects or distances. Our ideas get enlarged to "the utmost Bounds of all Bodies", "to the distance of the Sun, or remotest Star", beyond "all corporeal Being", and even beyond "all the measures of Time". These are impressive examples of enlargement.

1.2. Some Limitations

The language in these passages is rather confident, perhaps overconfident. There are limitations on the ideas we can form in these ways, limitations that affect the clarity or specific content of the ideas relevant to spirits and their intellectual world. For example, Locke says the idea of eternity is very confused.

Having frequently in our Mouths the Name *Eternity*, we are apt to think, we have a positive comprehensive *Idea* of it, which is as much to say, that there is no part of that Duration, which is not clearly contained in our *Idea*. 'Tis true, that he that thinks so, may have a clear *Idea* of Duration; he may also have a very clear *Idea* of a very great length of Duration; he may also have a clear *Idea* of the Comparison of that great one, with still a greater: But it not being possible for him to include in his *Idea* of any Duration, let it be as great as it will, the whole Extent together of a Duration, where he supposes no end, that part of his *Idea*, which is still beyond the Bounds of that large Duration, he represents to his own Thoughts, is very obscure and undetermined. (2.29.15)

The obscurity of this idea is matched by our efforts to form ideas of the very small, such as the particles or corpuscles of matter (2.29.16). In this section, he writes of the infinite divisibility of matter. We have clear ideas of division, part, whole but "only very obscure and confused *Ideas* of Corpuscles, or minute Bodies", which are to be further divided. We soon reach a point where the smallness is so far from "the perception of any of our Senses" that we cannot form a clear idea of the product. After a series of different examples of smaller and smaller products of division, he concludes: "So that, I think, when we talk of Division of Bodies *in infinitum*, our *Idea* of their distinct Bulks, which is the Subject and Foundation of Division, comes after a little progression, to be confounded, and almost lost in Obscurity". The obscurity comes when we try to form an idea of the corpuscles. In a process that is the reverse of enlarging, we can shrink our ideas to smaller and smaller objects but, as with eternity, we reach a point where idea-formation stops or becomes vague and unclear.

Are these remarks about the idea of corpuscles and the idea of eternity consistent with his account of the formation of ideas of God and spirits? Are those ideas clear and distinct or confused? He would not say we have a clear adequate idea of God, or of the natures of angels and spirits; but spirits are intelligent Beings, so I suppose we can assume that among other properties, they have some of the ones we as intelligent Beings possess. We simply have to predicate knowledge, etc., that we experience to those other intelligent Beings. Angels and separate spirits as intelligent Beings differ from the intelligent Beings Locke believes inhabit other mansions of this vast universe. Angels and separate spirits are devoid of matter, have no bodies (normally), while on his account those other Beings in other parts of the universe seem only to have refined and different sense organs and faculties from ours. It is easier to credit those Beings with some of our properties and operations, than it is to assign our faculties and mental operations of acquiring knowledge, feeling pleasure, and of experiencing happiness to the angels and separate spirits. The operation of enlarging ideas does not seem to yield clear and distinct ideas for understanding the existence of such spirits. The one property that does seem applicable to those spirits, as also to God, is knowledge. Perhaps power might work as well, although to enlarge that idea leaves it unclear just what angel-power is, how it is wielded, or on what objects it is directed. Happiness and pleasure have, as I have suggested, their own difficulty of conception. Just what is a happy angel or a happy spirit, to say nothing of a happy God, is unclear. The nature of their happiness is also obscure. So I think we have to conclude that Locke's efforts to explain how we can form clear or semi-clear and intelligible ideas of spirits and their properties is not entirely successful.

Locke agrees with this assessment of his efforts, at least with reference to "different *Species of Angels*": we are not able to "frame distinct specifick *Ideas* of them" (3.6.11). He explains what 'specific' ideas would be, ideas "of their different Natures, Conditions, States, Powers, and several Constitutions, wherein they agree or differ from one another, and from us. And therefore, in what concerns their different Species and Properties, we are under an absolute ignorance" (4.3.27).[5]

2. Conceivable, Intelligible

It is one thing to be ignorant of the species and properties of spirits, or to conjecture about the nature and existence of them. It is quite another to form clear and distinct ideas of them. I remarked in chapter 3 that when Locke talks of conceiving such Beings, he does not provide us with an analysis of the mental act of conceiving. To conceive of something requires, I think on his account, our having an idea of what we conceive. If we have, as he admits, obscure and unclear ideas of certain features of angels, such as their happiness, or the ways in which they differ from us, does that not affect our conception of them? Can we be said to conceive of something without having a clear idea of it?

When we search the text for what Locke says he can conceive, we find a variety of conceivables, from the idea of the solidity of body being that whereby we conceive bodies to fill space, or that the ideas of secondary qualities are produced in the same way as primary qualities, to other uses that express beliefs. The instances of 'conceive' that are most relevant to deciding whether Locke's account of angels and spirits is intelligible are examples that go beyond experience. There are a few such examples:

2.14.26—Whether the world is infinite or finite, both are equally conceivable.

2.15.4—We "easily conceive in GOD infinite Duration". In fact, "we cannot avoid doing so". This remark is preceded by some reflections on why some people are reluctant to "*admit, or suppose the Infinity of Space*", while "*every one* familiarly, and without the least hesitation, speaks of, and supposes Eternity". The reason given for the difference is somewhat obscure: "That Duration and Extension being used as names of affections belonging to other Beings, we easily conceive in GOD infinite Duration", but we tend to ascribe extension or expansion only to matter (here these terms are used interchangeably). This limit on the ascription of extension results in our assuming that space goes with body, and ends with body: no space without body, a claim he rejects. Section 3 of this chapter had said that God fills eternity, hence infinite duration. God also fills immensity, so why do we not easily conceive infinite space in God? The suggestion seems to be that we ought to be able to make a similar use of the idea of God's immensity to form the idea of, to conceive, infinite space. The notion of God filling or occupying all of time would seem to be easier to find intelligible than the notion of God, an immaterial Being, filling all of space. The distinction between the expansion of bodies and the expansion of non-material Beings is crucial for this example.

2.15.12—We "can conceive the eternal Duration of the Almighty far different from that of Man, or any other finite Being". So will man and other finite Beings have eternal duration? The explanation for the difference in conceiving the eternal duration of man (if that is what he is saying) and the eternal duration of God is that "Man comprehends not in his Knowledge, or Power, all past and future things", so the idea of the eternal duration of man in the next life is constricted by the limitations of our knowledge and experience. The same is true of all finite Beings who may "far exceed Man in Knowledge and Power, yet are no more than the meanest Creature, in comparison with God himself". Just who these other finite Beings are, Locke does not say. Are they higher on the chain of being? These remarks are fascinating if a bit unclear. Whether they shed any light on the claim that we can conceive infinite duration, form an idea of it, I am not sure.

2.23.19—We "may certainly conceive a distance, and a change of distance between two Spirits; and so conceive their Motion, their approach, or removal, one from another". This example rests on a principle that no thing can be or act where it is not. Hence, if spirits can act, they must be able to move, even though the kind of expansion spirits, even our souls, have is different from the extension of bodies. Similarly, the notion of spirits and souls moving would seem to require a different interpretation from our experience of bodies moving away from or towards us.

About his soul, Locke remarks that "my Soul being a real Being, as well as my Body, is certainly as capable of changing distance with any other Body, or Being, as Body it self; and so is capable of Motion" (2.23.19). This notion is reinforced in the next section: "Every one finds in himself, that his Soul can think, will, and operate on his Body, in the place where that is; but cannot operate on a Body, or in a place, an hundred Miles distant from it". Does he want to say the soul can operate on bodies other than its body, even a body near or next to its own body? There is some ambiguity in this sentence. When he continues, it seems to be the soul's body (the body of the soul) that he means. No one can "imagine [conceive?], that his Soul can think, or move a Body at *Oxford*, whilst he is at *London*; and cannot but know, that being [vitally] united to his Body, it constantly changes place all the whole Journey, between *Oxford* and *London*, as the Coach, or Horse does, that carries him". The 'him' in this passage is the man, the physical man. The man, the coach, and the horse have a different kind of reality, a different ontic status, from that of souls, so to say the coach carries the soul as it does the man, overlooks this important fact. It certainly is true that I cannot move a chair in Oxford when I am in London, so if we allow that it is the soul that moves our body and chairs, it would be true to say the soul is unable to move the chair in Oxford when it is in London.

Whether we find intelligible the notions of the soul moving objects, the soul being in a place, having an extension (expansion), or the soul moving from place to place, will depend upon our accepting at least two notions (or one notion and one principle): that the soul moves the body it inhabits, and that no thing (Being) can be or act where it is not.[6]

2.27.15: We may be able "without any difficulty to conceive, the same Person at the Resurrection, though in a Body not exactly" as the one we have in this life. This example may be the least controversial, since we are familiar with the same person in this life having different bodily forms, as with the young child, the adult, and the old man. Where difficulty confronts us is with the idea of the bodily form in what I assume is a non-material domain, the domain of God, Angels and Spirits.

Do these examples give us any information about the nature of conceiving? How do we determine whether we have conceived of something? One man's conception may be another's inconceivable! Some of these examples rest on basic notions that Locke accepted, such as that immaterial spirits have a kind of extension, or the principle of no action at a distance, or even that it is the soul that acts. So we can understand how some of what he finds conceivable is a function of prior notions. Whether this is the case for all that he finds conceivable may not be so clear, but I think we can say the examples so far do not provide us with a general criterion for intelligibility.

Will the examples of what is not conceivable (there are a number in the *Essay*) give us any guidance in our quest for a principle or criterion of intelligible or conceivable? The examples of what is not conceived fall into two groups: (1) what is impossible to conceive and, (2) what cannot be conceived. There is another group that may be seen as between these two and what can be and is conceived, but with difficulty: (3) what is hard to conceive.

2.1. The Impossible

1.3.2: Locke argues that there are no "moral Principles, wherein all Men do agree". He remarks that "*Justice,* and keeping of Contracts" are accepted by most men, even by outlaws, but the latter only follow them as rules of convenience, not as innate moral rules. It is impossible to conceive that they take them as universal innate principles since, while they may treat their fellow highway-men that way, they then rob and plunder the next honest man they come across. The assumption is that if a principle is innate, it will be followed by all men.

1.3.11: If there were innate moral rules imprinted on the minds of men, whole nations of men would not publicly reject and renounce "what every one of them, certainly and infallibly, knew to be a Law". It is impossible to conceive that they would renounce what they knew as infallible truths. This and the previous example simply draw out the implications of the claim for innate moral principles imprinted on the minds of all men. If you accept the innatist's claim, then exceptions falsify the claim. It is impossible to conceive exceptions if you accept that claim.

4.10.10: Thinking Matter. "For it is as impossible to conceive, that ever bare incogitative Matter should produce a thinking intelligent Being, as that nothing should of it self produce Matter". Another example in this section says "it is impossible to conceive that Matter either with or without Motion could have originally in and from it self Sense, Perception, and Knowledge". Locke is expressing his own belief here. The fact that there were some who at least tried to make thought a property of some matter, only suggests that what he finds inconceivable may not be so considered by others. Of course, under certain conditions Locke prescribed, God could have attached thought to the brain. I assume that Locke would say he was able to conceive this possibility.

2.2. The Cannot

2.15.12: We "cannot conceive any Duration without Succession, nor can put it together in our Thoughts, that any Being does now exist to Morrow, or possess at once more than the present moment of Duration". This is a rather obscure example. Two claims are made in this remark. One is what I take to be some kind of conceptual truth: if some Being exists now, that Being cannot at the same time exist tomorrow. The second claim is puzzling, it seems to say we cannot think of any being having a duration that extends to more than the present moment, a claim that does not sound like something Locke would say. As we have seen, he further remarks that "we can conceive of the eternal Duration of the Almighty", so perhaps what cannot be conceived is the eternal duration of finite Beings, and the 'to Morrow' may refer to the next life of man.

2.21.73: The question here is, what is the force or power of objects that cause sensible ideas in us? Locke's comment is that "we cannot conceive any thing else, to be in any sensible Object, whereby it produces different *Ideas* in us, but the different Bulk, Figure, Number, Texture, and Motion of its insensible Parts". Malebranche did not have any difficulty in conceiving that God causes our ideas.

2.23.4: Ideas of Substance. The ideas of corporeal substances, such as a horse or stone, consist of a collection of sensible qualities. Because "we cannot conceive, how they should subsist alone, nor one in another, we suppose them existing in, and supported by some common subject".

3.6.11: Names of substances, re God. In his excellence and perfection, God infinitely exceeds "what our narrow Understandings can conceive of him". This is more of a limitation on conception than a clear indication of what cannot be conceived.

4.2.1: A man "cannot conceive himself capable of a greater Certainty, than to know that any *Idea* in his Mind is such, as he perceives it to be . . ." His examples are non-informative truths such as, that white is not black, or a circle is not a triangle.

4.3.29: We cannot conceive that the relation of "a right-lined Triangle" to the sum of its angles could be changed or subject to some arbitrary power.

4.10.19: "We cannot conceive how anything but impulse of Body, can move Body". However, he modifies this claim, first by saying our inability to conceive in this case is no reason to deny that there may be other causes that move body. In fact, as he explains, we experience in ourselves "in all our voluntary Motions" of our body, the "free Action or Thought of our own Minds" moving our body.[7]

2.3. The Hard to Conceive

1.4.8: It is "hard to conceive, how there should be innate Moral Principles, without an innate *Idea* of a *Deity*".
2.1.11: It is "hard to conceive, that any thing should think, and not be conscious of it". Did Descartes, as a thing that thinks, manage to conceive that he thought when he was not conscious of thinking?
2.15.11: It is "near as hard to conceive any Existence, or to have an *Idea* of any real Being, with a perfect Negation of all manner of Expansion; as it is, to have the *Idea* of any real Existence, with a perfect Negation of all manner of Duration". Again perhaps a conceptual truth: if any thing exists, it endures for some time.
2.27.21: It is "hard to conceive, that *Socrates* the same individual Man should be two Persons".
4.19.10: It is "hard to conceive how there can be a Revelation to any one of what he knows already". This sounds like another simple conceptual truth.

The section in which this last example of what is hard to conceive contains several references to spirits. Locke is discussing the claims of some 'enthusiasts' that they have revelations from God via an internal light. "These Men have, they say, clear Light, and they see; They have an awaken'd Sense, and they feel: This cannot, they are sure, be disputed them. For when a Man says he sees or he feels, no Body can deny it him, that he does so" (4.19.10). Locke puts to them this question: "This seeing is it the perception of the Truth of the Proposition, or of this, that it is a Revelation from GOD?" Locke suggests that the feeling is an inclination or fancy or, as they believed, "the Spirit of GOD moving them". What is lacking in these claims is some way of telling that what they see or feel is a revelation from God. Even if they think some truth has been given them in some unnatural way, that does not show it is a revelation from God, "Because there be Spirits, which, without being divinely commissioned, may excite those *Ideas* in me, and lay them in such order before my Mind, that I may perceive their Connexion". We need to know that God is the revealer of the truth "and that what I take to be a Revelation is certainly put into my Mind by him, and is not an Illusion drop'd in by some other Spirit, or raised by my own phancy".

These examples of what can or cannot be conceived are important for the expression of Locke's thought on a number of the topics discussed in the *Essay*. He uses the various claims as a way of refuting a counter claim, as a means for talking about God or his revelation, a rejection of materialism, a defense of empty space, even for his notion of the motion and expansion of spirits. He does not address the question we might pose: how does he decide that something is conceivable, or how does he determine that his account of the domain of God, Angels and Spirits is intelligible?

3. Other Accounts of Spirits

Besides forming ideas of God and spirits by enlarging the qualities and powers we experience in our own case, we apparently acquire information about spirits by other means. The reference to specific ideas of different species of angels begins by saying "we are told" that there are such species (3.6.11). There is no indication as to who it was that gave this information about angels. He may be referring to the Bible, although, while there are multiple references in the Old Testament to 'angel', as in 'angel of the Lord', a few to 'angels', I cannot discover any mention of species of angels or of species of spirits. So the source of this information remains obscure.[8] Locke did have in his library two books about spirits, but they were both published in 1694, too late to be the source of Locke's account of spirits. These two, however, are useful for giving us some indication of what other writers were saying about this interesting topic. One of these was an elaborate four-volume work, *Le Monde enchanté. ou Examen des communs sentimens touchant les Esprits, leur nature, leur pouvoir, leur administration et leurs opérations* by Balthasar Bekker. The other book is by Richard Burthogge, *An Essay upon Reason & the Nature of Spirits*.[9] A brief examination of Burthogge's book (which was dedicated to Locke) may serve to show some of the differences. A few remarks about Bekker's curious book are also relevant.

3.1. Burthogge

Burthogge's references to spirits are rather different from those of Locke's, although there are some similarities. His discussion ranges from the Mosaical Spirit, the subtle matter that pervades the universe (a notion associated with Cudworth and Henry More, in *An Essay upon Reason and the Nature of Spirits*, p. 124), to apparitions and ghosts (p. 177). Whereas Locke looks for an immaterial cause of gravity, Burthogge invokes spirits to account for "Operations we are certain of, which cannot be Accounted for but by supposing such Agents" (p. 177). The operations he has in mind are "the strange Performances of Witches and Wizards" (p. 178), strange premonitions (p. 197), and apparitions (p. 211). When, in his *Education*, Locke urges the tutor to instill "into the Minds of Children a notion and belief in Spirits", he cautions: "I would not have Children troubled whilst young with Notions of Spirits, whereby they should receive early Impressions of Goblins, Spectres, and Apparitions" (§§190–91, pp. 245–46). He dismisses those notions, saying they are used by children's "Maids, and those about them" as a way of frightening them "into Compliance with their Orders". Besides "subjecting their Minds to Frights, fearful Apprehensions, Weakness, and Superstitions", there is another more important negative result from these notions: they cause those who have been subjected to them to "throw away the thoughts of all Spirits together, and so run into the other worse extream" (§191, p. 246). The other extreme would be to think only of matter and corporeal things. He voices the same warning in the *Essay:* "The *Ideas* of *Goblines* and *Sprights* have really no more to do with Darkness than Light; yet let but a foolish Maid inculcate these often on the Mind of a Child, and raise them there together, possibly he shall never be able to separate them again so long as he lives, but Darkness shall ever afterwards bring with it those frightful *Ideas*" (2.33.10). Those goblins, specters, and apparitions are not the spirits that Locke cites so often in his *Essay.* So Locke's orientation towards spirits, as well as the kinds of spirits mentioned, differs from those discussed by Burthogge.

In dedicating his book to Locke, Burthogge probably had in mind Locke's attention to reason and the cognitive faculties of the mind, about which Burthogge writes in his *Essay,* rather than the spirits that he also discusses. His interests in spirits is more with their supposed appearance to men than with any detailed account of their nature. However, there are some passages in which he does characterize some features and powers of spirits. They are described as 'intellectual Beings', as in Locke (p. 171). Oddly, Burthogge classes spirits as animals! In fact, there are two classes of animals, visible and invisible. "By invisible Animals, I mean Angels good and bad, which I call Ætherial Animals, as also those Æreal ones (some Ludicrous, some Torvous) that are called Genii" (p. 162; cf. p. 176).[10] Angels and other spirits are incorporeal, but they may also have some refined matter, so they can be said to be both incorporeal and corporeal (pp. 164–65). They are said to be 'vitally united' to matter, a phrase that we have seen Locke used (p. 168). Matter is apparently required if spirits are to be distinguished as to kinds: "were Spirits Absolutely Pure and Simple, without any Admission of Matter, there could be no Distinction among them in respect of Kinds" (p. 166). It is the refined matter of spirits that also individuates them (p. 167). There are, he says, "several Species; Angels in Heaven, and Devils out of it; and perhaps a Lower sort of Spirits than those we commonly call

Devils" (p. 234). He even speaks of their having 'Spiritual Bodies' (p. 169). Later in his essay, Burthogge speaks of "Real Appearing" when spirits "present themselves to some of the Outward senses, and (particularly to the Eye) in some thing that does Really Affect it" (p. 223). Such appearances are "generally thought to be performed, either by their assuming of Bodies that are already prepared, or by Figuring the Air, or some other Elementary Substance into the shapes in which they appear" (p. 224).[11]

He also refers to the chain of being in terms very similar to those Locke used. "There are no Vacuities, or Gaps in Nature, in respect of Species, no Jumps or Leaps, but all in orderly Gradation", and he continues by citing the usual examples of minerals, vegetables, fishes, flying fishes, lambs, bats, etc. (pp. 248–49).[12]

3.2. Bekker

Bekker's four-volume work had a much wider circulation and even notoriety than that of Burthogge. In fact, Bekker's work, published originally in Dutch, stirred controversy almost from its first appearance. The first two volumes came out in 1691, and the entire work was translated into several other languages; an abridged English edition was made under the title *The World Bewitched*. As I have indicated, Locke owned the French edition, four volumes published in 1694. Locke may have learned about Bekker from his Dutch correspondent, Philippus van Limborch, as early as 1691. In a letter to Locke dated 21/31 July 1691, Limborch suggested that Locke's *Essay* "would be most profitable reading, especially for those people who build an entire system on some concept that is not sufficiently full and distinct, as if it were full, distinct, and adequate".[13] Men suppose, Limborch went on to say, "that they have apprehended a thing fully and adequately, whereas they have only an imperfect concept of it". He then cited Bekker as an example: "We have a living proof of this at the present moment in our city. A minister of the Public Church of this city, by name Balthasar Bekker, a doctor of theology, has published a book concerning the existence of spirits. In it he attempts to show that evil daemons, or devils as we call them, never assail or have assailed men or infested their bodies; that they did not lead the first of mankind astray or tempt the Lord Jesus, and much else that is contrary to the common opinion of Christians". On good angels, Limborch says that Bekker does not ascribe to them "what the Christian world unanimously believes is ascribed to them in Scripture. Of those many passages of Scripture which speak of angels good as well as bad he has a widely different explanation".

Limborch has much more to say about the contents of Bekker's book, but he also says that Bekker was imprudent, and he tells Locke that "By the publication of his book he has provoked harsh judgments on the part of his fellows, some of whom do not hesitate to decry him as an advocate of atheism; indeed, I seriously fear that unless he makes a recantation he may be deprived of his ministry and functions in the Church. So dangerous is it to contradict a received opinion of theologians". So Locke was apprised of the general nature of Bekker's book in 1691. Whether he had looked at a copy that early, we cannot say. Nor can we determine what his opinion was of the book, even after he purchased a copy, presumably in 1694 or later. There is one possibly positive remark he makes in a letter to Limborch of November 14, 1691. He asks Limborch "What was done in the end with that doctor of theology who taught such marvelous things about angels in his book on the existence of spirits? Has he not experienced his brethen's zeal for religion, truth, and orthodoxy?"[14] Does this remark suggest that Locke had seen a copy (he did not read Dutch), or is he just relying on what Limborch told him? In 1692, Limborch refers to Bekker's 'paradox about angels', but he does not explain what the paradox was. He describes in great detail what has happened to Bekker, the trial and condemnation.[15]

In that same letter, Limborch mentions another earlier book on demons, *The Doctrine of Devils, proved to be the grand apostasy of these later years. An Essay tending to rectifie those undue notions and apprehensions men have about dæmons and evil spirits*, by N. Orchard (1676). Limborch says that Bekker "follows his opinions and contends with various arguments taken from that pamphlet, though he has much else to say about dæmons". And Limborch remarks again on the imprudence of Bekker: many of his doctrines give "an opportunity to profane men for finding fault with sundry narratives in Scripture". Again, he goes into details about Bekker's doctrines. So clearly by early 1692 Locke had learned much about the contents of Bekker's book, especially the fact that Bekker was in trouble with the Church.

From Limborch's account and from the controversy Bekker's book had aroused in Holland, it does not sound as if the discussions of angels and spirits there had much in common with Locke's account. That impression is reinforced by a glance at the table of contents for each volume. The subtitle of volume 1 says he will examine the "commun sentimens touchant les Esprits, leur nature, leur pouvoir, leur administration, & leur opérations". That volume consists of a rather detailed historical account of the views of various ancient groups, including Christians (both Catholics and Protestants) of more recent times. There is very little independent analysis of those items listed in the sub-title. Judging from the table of contents of volume 2, that volume promises to be more relevant to Locke's account and use of spirits. However, there is very little about the nature and operation of spirits. He gives the standard definition of spirits as incorporeal, created substances, insisting that they have no affinity with bodies, that is, the two substances of spirits and bodies have none of their properties in common.[16] He describes spirits as 'creatures', the term indicating that they are caused by something higher, i.e., God.[17] In a number of passages, he speaks of the human soul as a spirit—it is that which thinks.[18] While attached to the body, it is not as pure or perfect as when it exists separate from it.[19] Several sections in chapter 5 discuss the possibility that human souls inhabit other bodies when their original ones die. Throughout, he is skeptical about the existence of other spirits, but there is extended discussion of angels and devils, the beliefs about them held by many, especially Christians.[20] The list of beliefs enumerated by Bekker in volume 1 is rather stunning, from the great numbers of good and bad angels and sprits, to the powers of both, and the very specific ways the devil intervenes in human lives, directly and by illusions and false appearances.[21]

Bekker does have an interesting notion of the place of spirits. While a body cannot be in two places at the same time, spirits can occupy several places at the same time. His concept of being in a place for spirits is different from that of Locke. Spirits are not in a place on their own, as it were, but only in relation to that on which they act or operate.[22] The actions he has in mind are cognitive acts. Chapter 3 of this volume explains that we should not ask where a spirit is, only where it acts.[23] For example, the place of the soul can be said to be where its body is, since that is where it acts on or with the body. But if "the soul dreams of persons or things in other places, near or far, it is also in those places".[24] If we wish to ascribe the place of the soul as the place where some body other than our own body is located, the soul does not have to see that body, only think of it. If Bekker dreams of London and Paris in order to compare them, then his soul is in London, Paris, and the village where he resides. Even if I think of the sun and stars, my soul is there also. I or my soul (I guess the soul is proxy for the man) is where my thoughts are. In this way, more than one soul can occupy the same place. He gives the example of King William in his ship, presumably on his way to England. The many people in Holland who think of him or wish him well can be said to be with him in the ship.[25]

When Bekker says the soul is where it acts or operates, the only actions or operations he allows are cognitive ones. As Wiep van Bunge remarks about bodiless spirits, all that they can do is to think, they are, as it were, self-contained.[26] Limborch's way of putting this point about Bekker's account is to say that thought "cannot operate in any way outside itself; its operation is wholly immanent". Hence he concludes that "angels cannot operate in any way either on our soul or on our body; the soul can, indeed, operate upon the body with which it is united, but on nothing else".[27]

Bekker's main objective seems to have been to attack the notion that spirits could intervene in human life and action. He explains that his method is to use reason and the Scriptures, but it was his interpretation of the Scriptures that got him into trouble, quite apart from his conclusions. Coming after the first Dutch edition, this French version contains in volume 1 a long summary, an 'Abrégé', of all the volumes. The bulk of the volumes consists of long discussions of passages from the Scriptures. Andrew Fix explains that "In his book Bekker attacked the popular belief that the devil plagued people and influenced temporal affairs by means of evil spirits, ghosts, and witches. He saw these beliefs as even more harmful than fear of comets because people lost their lives over witchcraft. In addition, belief in evil spirits was not just a superstition of the ignorant".[28] Fix goes on to remark that "Despite the fact that belief in witchcraft and magic met with growing skepticism in educated circles after 1650, belief in spirits remained a part of the world view of many educated Christians". The rest of his 1989 article and chapter 5 of his book contain an account of a number of other writers in Holland who wrote about spirits and angels. Apparently there was a rather extensive number of books and articles on the topic. How much if any of this literature was known to Locke, I do not know, but it is clear that, aside from some common notions of spirits (that they are incorporeal, they may possibly exist, the rational soul is that which thinks), Locke's interest in and use of angels and spirits differs fundamentally from the beliefs Bekker attacks and from the other writers in Holland discussed by Fix.[29]

Conclusion

Locke is cautious in his statements about spirits, speaking often of opinions or of what may be possible. For example, 4.3.17 speaks of "possibly innumerable, kinds of nobler Beings" and 4.3.27 refers to "that infinite number of *Spirits* that may be, and probably" do exist but which are remote from our knowledge. *Essay* 4.3.29 confirms his doubts about a science of bodies and of spiritual Beings, an a priori and deductive science (see also 4.7.7 and 4.11.12). Another section speaks of opinions only about "The Existence, Nature, and Operations of finite immaterial Beings without us" (4.16.12). He gives examples of "Spirits, Angels, Devils, *etc.*" What the 'etc.' covers is not indicated.

Striking about Locke's account of spirits (his suggestion about their nature and properties, the formation of ideas of spirits and angels, and what can be and cannot be conceived about them) is how integrated these are into his analysis of the origin of simple and complex ideas, the workings of the faculties of the mind, the scope and limitations of human knowledge and understanding. His discussion and analysis of some of the main topics in the *Essay* uses angels and spirits as examples or illustrations: for example, his explication of some of the properties of minds and souls, the account of memory, as an illustration of what certain knowledge of body would be, as part of his explication of space and duration. In these many ways wherein spirits appear in the *Essay* with specific doctrines of that work, I suspect that Locke's references to and discussion of spirits probably differ from all other contemporary accounts of spirits. No other philosopher in the seventeenth and eighteenth centuries writing on knowledge, perception, and reality makes use of the chain of being, angels and spirits, to illustrate and explain their accounts. In fact, there does not seem to be any other text in those centuries that combines so effectively an account of the extent and limits of knowledge, the workings of the mind, the physiology of the body, the acquisition of ideas, the experimental science of nature, natural philosophy, moral theory, and a deep religious concern for the future life.

CHAPTER FIVE

SOULS THAT BECOME SPIRITS

Discussions of the soul in the *Essay* are mainly clustered around three main topics. The first in order of appearance is the discussion of innate ideas and principles (1.2–4). There Locke is using the language of those, mostly divines and other writers in England, who defended the claim. They talked of impressions on the soul, but there is no reason to think Locke did not accept the soul as part of a human Being. He talks of the faculties of the soul and he characterizes man as "a Creature, consisting of Soul and Body" (1.4.4). The second group of sections dealing with the soul of man concerns the claim that the soul always thinks, that thinking is the essence of the soul. Locke rejects this claim in an extended critique in a dozen long, sometimes dense sections (2.1.9–21).[1] The third extended discussion is in the chapter on identity and diversity in which personal identity is explicated (2.27.6, 14–16, 21, 27).

There are other chapters and sections in which some discussion of the soul occurs. References can be found to the rational soul, its immateriality and immortality, its role in thinking and acting, but there are few attempts made to explain what a human soul is.[2] In fact, Locke was concerned to argue that we do not know much about the soul, we think of it as an immaterial substance but we know nothing about its supposed substantiality. But ignorance about the nature of soul does not lead him to discard it from his account of man. The soul of man does not figure prominently in his analysis of human understanding, the accounts of perception, the formation of belief, or in his stress on the importance of experience and observation in reaching truth. Sometimes the soul is a silent partner in the activity of the mind, he often alternates between mind and soul. That alternative introduces an initial ambiguity about the roles of mind and soul, even whether these are the same. The "Epistle to the Reader" characterizes the understanding as "the most elevated Faculty of the Soul", saying it searches after truth, taking delight in that search. The same paragraph refers to the mind in its progress towards truth and knowledge. The mind relies on the faculty of the soul in that search (p. 6). When he turns to analyzing the claim for innate principles, he says the claim was that the principles were "stamped upon the Mind of Man", but it is the soul which receives those principles "in its very first Being" (1.2.1). Section 2 of this chapter repeats this claim, including saying that it is the soul, not the mind, that receives them. Is there a significant difference between 'stamped' and 'receives'? Perhaps 'receives' indicates that it is the soul that perceives or is aware of the innate principles which are then stamped on the mind. He does say thinking is the action of the soul, not its essence (2.19.4). But imprinting is also ascribed to the soul, so the distinction may not be firm. Section 5 finds him objecting that there is a contradiction in saying there are principles imprinted on the soul which the soul neither perceives nor understands. Section 27 of the first chapter says explicitly that these men suppose that the innate principles are "stamped immediately on the Soul". So in these statements of the innate claim, the stamping and imprinting is said to be on the mind in one passage but on the soul in others. The innatists may not have been as careful with language as he liked to be. Locke is stating the claims of the innatists and not attempting to clarify their language. For this reason we may not be able to draw any conclusions about his views on mind or soul from these passages. These passages do, however, have the same ambiguity as we find in the "Epistle to the Reader".

The soul has other faculties besides the understanding. Some faculties are characterized as "the reasoning Faculties of the Soul" (1.3.26). He does not name those faculties in this section but it is clear that he is speaking for himself in saying these faculties belong to the soul, not to the mind. When he moves into book 2 and begins to develop his alternative account, the ambiguity or ambivalence about mind and soul surfaces again. He refers to the operations of the mind, saying that the soul reflects on and considers those operations (2.1.4, line 14). But in line 26 he has the mind reflecting on those operations; the mind takes notice of them as well. The discussion of retention as a faculty of the mind has the mind attempting to retrieve some hidden idea, some forgotten idea. In doing so, the mind "turns, as it were, the Eye of the Soul upon" that idea. So here the soul functions in the service of the mind. Thus, the two are clearly distinct in this section (2.10.7). The soul discovers the idea that the mind sought. Other faculties of the mind are perception (2.9.1) and discerning (2.11.1). A later section (2.21.6) identifies the understanding and the will as faculties of the mind, but in the rest of the sentence he warns us not to take the term 'faculty' as indicating a real Being in the soul: "For when we say the *Will* is the commanding and superior Faculty of the Soul; that it is, or is not free; that it determines the inferior Faculties; that it follows the Dictates of the *Understanding*, etc.", we can easily be led to think of agents in the soul with a real Being. He does not say what the alternative way is for interpreting understanding and volition, but the implicit suggestion is that they are functions or operations of the mind or soul.

Locke was uncomfortable with the term 'faculty'. Frequently, he uses it in the sense of an ability, the abilities to discern, to collect, to abstract, to reason. Sometimes he prefers to speak of powers, e.g., the will as a "power of the Mind to determine its thought" (2.21.15). The danger he saw in treating faculties as real Beings is that they tend to get proliferated into useless and senseless notions, such as a walking faculty, a discerning faculty, a speaking faculty, etc. (2.21.17). In trying to sort out which faculties belong to the mind and which to the soul, we really are asking what are the actions, operations, and abilities of each. That he was unsure or imprecise about these assignments may indicate his uncertainty about what the mind is, if indeed it is different from the soul. We might find it more to our taste to say that those abilities and powers are abilities and powers of the man or the person. I do not think that would quite satisfy Locke, certainly not in regard to the soul, as we will see in a moment.

There are many more occurrences of 'mind' than of 'soul' throughout the *Essay*, and in his *Education* it is the mind that the tutor works with, not the soul. Soul is hardly mentioned there at all. Of the three topics where 'soul' is prominent in the *Essay*, the first two (the innate claim and the notion that thought is the essence of the soul and hence thinks always) are issues raised by others that he criticizes and rejects. The third topic of identity and diversity advances Locke's own account of personal identity. The soul is prominent in that discussion. But in that chapter, he is mainly concerned to separate the soul (at least the soul as substance) from the identity of person. The various puzzle cases do raise a number of possibilities about the relation of soul to the body and to the man, but it is difficult to discern what in those examples reveals Locke's beliefs about the soul.

1. Soul as Spirit

Where the soul comes into its own, where its importance emerges from the many topics of the *Essay*, concerns Locke's reference to the chain of being, angels and spirits, the second intellectual world, and man's concern for a future life. Then an interesting transformation takes place. No longer is the soul associated with the secular activity of the human mind: soul joins with the separate spirits. It even becomes one of those spirits. There is (as we have seen) one clear statement in 2.23.19 in which Locke says his soul is "a real Being, as well as my Body".[3] A real being that is immaterial but not, I think, intelligent or rational, as other spirits are, although the 1.3.26 passage does speak of the reasoning faculty of the soul. Perhaps that does make the soul rational. It apparently thinks, and it can move the body by thought. In this way it has active power as other spirits also have. Is the mind a real Being? Here is where an important difference appears between soul and mind. The mind is not, so far as I can determine from his text, a real Being, although it is far from clear just what the mind is. Perhaps it fades into the soul or, we may say, the soul absorbs some of the functions of the mind. As a real Being, the soul has a quite different status in Locke's ontology than does the mind. The real Being status opens the way for the soul to leave the body, perhaps exist apart from the body, or inhabit other bodies, as those puzzle cases of *Essay* 2.27 suggest. That status also readies the soul for immortality, not an immortality on its own, separate from the body it inhabited in this life, but as a component in the man, person, and body at the resurrection. The same status as a real Being also explains Locke's insistence that the soul moves and has a place, although again not on its own but as related to the body. The soul is "certainly as capable of changing distance with any other Body, or Being, as Body it self" (2.23.19). That section is one of several in which soul is used interchangeably with spirit.[4] He announces that "Spirits, as well as Bodies, cannot operate, but where they are", a principle (as I remarked in the previous chapter) of no action at a distance frequently found in books at that time. The next few sentences then use 'soul'; hence, it is clear that it is treated as the same as spirit. A number of other passages make the same linkage even more explicit. One such place is where Locke discusses the powers spirits may have. In the chapter on the idea of substance, he contrasts the power of body to communicate motion by impulse, a passive power, with the active power of souls, a power of *"exciting of Motion by Thought"* (2.23.28). 'Souls' becomes 'minds' in the next line. He admits that he does not know how "our Minds move or stop our Bodies by Thought", but we know thought does so: "We have by daily experience clear evidence of Motion produced both by impulse, and by thought; but the manner how, hardly comes within our comprehension; we are equally at a loss in both."[5] 'Soul' and 'mind' become 'spirit' in line 29. Locke suggests that active power is "the proper attribute of Spirits". For this reason, he conjectures "that created Spirits are not totally separate from Matter, because they are both active and passive". How he reaches the conclusion that spirits are both active and passive is not immediately clear. But he now introduces the notion of 'pure' spirit—spirit that is all and only active, i.e. God. There are finite beings such as ourselves that are both active and passive, beings with matter and thought. Perhaps some of the other spirits are also active and passive, although none of them has a body (normally).

What I find curious, even intriguing, is the shift Locke makes in these passages from soul and mind to spirit, especially to the plural form 'spirits'. It was not uncommon at that time to speak of soul as a spirit. Locke does so in other passages, but in the context of his account of the chain of being with other spirits above man, we need to ask 'is the spirit of man one of the spirits on that chain?' Locke certainly located man on the chain, along with animals of all sorts. But is there a suggestion in the 2.23.28 section that part of man is, as it were, a member of the rank of spirits, although low on the chain? He returns to the question of the power of spirits later in 4.3.17. There he says again that *"we are much more in the dark in reference to* [the powers of] *Spirits"*. What few ideas we have come from "reflecting on the Operations of our own Souls within us". He then changes from 'souls' to 'spirits': "But how inconsiderable a rank the Spirits that inhabit our Bodies hold amongst those various, and possibly innumerable, kinds of nobler Beings; and how far short they come of the Endowments and Perfections of Cherubims, and Seraphims, and infinite sorts of Spirits above us, is what by a transient hint, in another place, I have offered to my Reader's Consideration." However, it seems that the soul as one of the spirits is different in kind from other spirits. Perhaps it is one of the species Locke mentions elsewhere, a kind that does not have a 'personality' (as the *OED* definition cited in chapter 3 said). Other spirits have faculties like ours but they are more powerful, and they also are 'person-like' (using 'person' in the ordinary, not in Locke's special sense). Soul is not, I think, quite person-like, although it thinks and reasons and moves bodies.

There is a struggle (some might be tempted to characterize this as an Hegelian struggle) between soul and the man, the soul having some of the faculties and operations we ordinarily think of as belonging to the man, the individual, not to the mind or soul. It is as if the soul seeks to take over the individual. Locke says that we look on the soul as ourselves, but there is still a distinction between the man and the soul. That distinction affects the immortality of both. Immortality of the soul-spirit (if I can refer to it in this way) and immortality of man, or man as a person, seem to be quite different.[6]

The *Essay* 4.3.17 passage is quite clear: the spirits that inhabit our bodies are located on the chain of being. Locke does not often speak of souls inhabiting our bodies, but there is one place where he does, 2.27.15. Moreover, 2.27.27 refers to the thing in us that thinks, leaving it unclear whether the 'thing' is soul or spirit. Neither of these references contain the 'transient hint' referred to in 4.3.17. The most likely candidate for 'another place' is in 3.6.12 where he sketches the gradations on the chain of being. But that section does not mention the spirits that inhabit our bodies. It does speak of "*Species* of intelligent Creatures above us" and others below us. He also says "there should be far more *Species* of intelligent Creatures above us" than below. It is 'us', humans (not the spirits that inhabit our bodies) that are located on the chain in this passage (see also §§22, 23). So if this is the place that a 'transient hint' is supposed to be, it does not say what Locke said in section 4.3.17. I do not think he ever speaks of the soul being located on the chain of being, but if soul and spirit are interchangeable, there may be little significance in the difference of terms. But unless he means to identify the spirits or souls that inhabit our bodies with the man or person, we have a major change in his account of man. If soul is one of the spirits on the chain, this

4.3.17 passage departs from the many other passages of the *Essay* that describe the workings of the mind and, to a lesser extent, the soul. Man's duality of mind and matter now acquires another duality, that of two locations on the chain: the body being placed somewhat lower than the spirit that inhabits that body, the spirit in turn being lower than other nobler spirits. There is another fascinating passage late in the *Essay* that picks up this same notion, moving the spirits of men up the chain. There, he refers to intuitive knowledge, the certainty we have about some truth as soon as we become aware of it. These truths are known without the use of discursive reasoning: they are known by what he describes as "a superior, and higher Degree of Evidence" (4.17.14). "And such, if I may guess at Things unknown, I am apt to think, that Angels have now, and the Spirits of just Men made perfect, shall have, in a future State, of Thousands of Things, which now, either wholly escape our Apprehensions, or which, our short-sighted Reason having got some faint Glimpse of, we, in the Dark, grope after".[7]

So the spirits that inhabit our bodies will be made perfect if the man is just, at the Great Day, a rather radical move up the chain! The 'guess' in this passage is that the soul-spirits will have intuitive knowledge or certainty of many things when they move up the chain. So now those soul-spirits seem to be cognizers, perhaps person-like after all. In this passage, what is it that is made perfect, the men or the spirits? I think it has to be the soul-spirits. As they move up the chain, they become more perfect. In doing so, they acquire more of the person-like characteristics.[8]

2. The Relation of Man, Soul, and Body

There are several questions that need to be raised if we are to reach an understanding of this passage. Foremost of the questions is 'what is the relation between the spirits that inhabit our bodies and those other important items, man, self, person and body?' Section 2.27.27 about "the thinking thing, that is in us" further said, "we look on [it] as our *selves*". Section 25 refers to that "which is conscious in us". It is not clear whether what is conscious in us is the same as the thinking thing that is in us, but 2.27.14 says quite firmly that it is the immaterial spirit that thinks in us. So the immaterial spirit is the thinking thing. Moreover, that spirit seems to be what a man calls himself, suggesting that the immaterial spirit is the self, or, since it is a man, not a person in this example, perhaps this remark only makes the immaterial spirit the man. We can reach this conclusion by reflecting on ourselves, but how reflection could lead to the double conclusion, that there is a thinking thing in us and that the immaterial spirit is the self (or the man), is not at all obvious. That section also identifies the soul as the immaterial spirit.

2.1. Sameness of Man

Section 21 of this chapter may echo section 14, although section 21 is a polemical one, so it is difficult to extract Locke's own views from the discussion. He wants to defend his suggestion that "the same Man" could be two persons. He offers three definitions of same man. The three definitions or characterizations may reveal something about Locke's thinking, but none of the three matches the definition of same man that he gives at 2.27.6: "a participation of the same continued Life, by constantly fleeting particles of Matter, in succession vitally united to the same organized Body". It is physical man that is described in this definition. The definitions of 2.27.21 are rather different. The first of these three defines "same individual *Man*" as "the same individual, immaterial, thinking Substance"; there is no mention of physical man. An alternative is "the same numerical Soul". Locke's comment on the first definition is brief and cryptic: "For by the First of them, it must be allowed possible that a Man born of different Women, and in distant times, may be the same Man" (2.27,21). The hidden premise is that the soul, the thinking thing, has the consciousness that makes personal identity. In these sections (20–22) the referent of the first person 'I' is to the man or the person, but for purposes of his argument here, he does not need the distinction between man and person. The reason for saying the man (i.e. soul) born of one woman is the same man or person as the soul born of another woman is presumably that they have the same consciousness—consciousness of the same events and actions. Thus, the soul is individuated by consciousness.

The second definition is "the same Animal" with no reference to an immaterial soul. The third simply adds an immaterial soul to the second definition, substituting 'spirit' for 'soul': "the same immaterial Spirit united to the same Animal". The example Locke uses to test the second and third definitions is that of "*Socrates* in this Life, and after it". He makes a strange remark: Socrates "cannot be the same Man [in this life and after] but by the same consciousness". Sameness of immaterial spirit will not preserve the sameness of the man. The inclusion of 'animal' here may capture the 'physical man' of the definition in 2.27.6, but the point of the first and third definitions in 2.27.21 is to introduce the soul and immateriality as part of the defining features of 'same man', with consciousness considered as a function of the immaterial spirit. It is not just the presence of the immaterial spirit that protects the sameness of man: consciousness has to function as well. So, it seems, the spirits of just men will not identify the men at the resurrection, although it is one of the properties or functions of spirits that they preserve the sameness of men. Locke gives no explanation here for the appeal to consciousness in his comments about sameness of man, but in section 15 he simply asserts that "the Soul alone in the change of Bodies [at the resurrection],[9] would scarce to any one, but to him that makes the Soul the *Man,* be enough to make the same *Man.*" Section 16 is more specific: "but though the same immaterial Substance, or Soul does not alone, where-ever it be, and in whatsoever State, make the same Man; yet 'tis plain consciousness, as far as ever it can be extended" is what makes the same man. Is Locke one of those who makes the soul the man?

These last two comments seem to dismiss the idea that the soul makes the same man, at least, as I have just said, not by itself. Since he links soul with immaterial substance in the comment from section 16, that may be the reason soul does not make the same man, given Locke's general reluctance about substance. However, section 27, three sections from the end of the chapter, seems to affirm his belief: "But taking, as we ordinarily now do, (in the dark concerning these Matters) the Soul of a Man, for an immaterial Substance, independent from Matter, and indifferent alike to it all, there can from the Nature of things, be no Absurdity at all, to suppose that the same Soul may, at different times be united to different Bodies, and with them make up, for that time, one Man". Now it is the combination of soul and body that makes or constitutes a man. Soul alone does not make a man. The presence of a soul is necessary for the sameness of a man, but the sameness of a man does not require the sameness of a soul. This passage also seems to suggest that Locke, perhaps as an ordinary man, did accept the soul as a substance. If so, he was serious in his controversy with Stillingfleet in saying he had not discarded substance out of the world, even though some of his statements in the *Essay* may seem to support the Bishop's suspicions. This passage is also consistent with the soul being one of the spirits, in the sense that it is indifferent to and independent of matter, the body. By using the word 'we', Locke associates himself with others, the ordinary beliefs about the soul. These beliefs do not affect his analysis of personal identity, in which sameness of soul is irrelevant. He also wants to separate the soul from the identity of man. This is why he tries to make sameness of consciousness the source of man's identity or, as he labels it in §21, "*Humane Identity*". So consciousness identifies or individuates the soul, the man, and the person. Consciousness may be the link between these three items, making them one unit.

Section 27 is also important for its inventory of what we do not know about the nature of the soul or the thing that thinks in us. Locke begins the section by confessing that he is

> apt enough to think I have in treating of this Subject made some Suppositions that will look strange to some Readers, and possibly they are so in themselves. But yet I think,

they are such, as are pardonable in this ignorance we are in of the Nature of that thinking thing, that is in us, and which we look on as our *selves*. Did we know what it was, or how it was tied to a certain System of fleeting Animal Spirits; or whether it could, or could not perform its Operations of Thinking and Memory out of a Body organized as ours is; and whether it has pleased God, that no one such Spirit shall ever be united to any but one such Body, upon the right Constitution of whose Organs its Memory should depend, we might see the Absurdity of some of those Suppositions I have made. (2.27.27)

Now the question is: 'can sameness of consciousness make and preserve the identity of both the man and the person?' A subsidiary question is: 'what is it that survives the change from this life to the next? what appears at the resurrection?' The resurrection is not discussed in the *Essay*, but it is mentioned in a few passages besides 2.27.15. In that section it is the person that is at the resurrection. It is the person also in 1.4.5. Two other passages simply refer to the resurrection of the dead, Locke's preferred locution when debating Bishop Stillingfleet (4.3.29 and 4.17.23). There are three candidates for what or who appears on the Great Day: the person, the man, or the Spirit that had inhabited the man's body in this life. From what we have just seen in his discussion in sections 15 and 21, there may be a problem about consciousness being able to determine the identity of the three candidates. At least, it is not easy to understand how consciousness could play all three roles without diluting the importance of consciousness in constituting personal identity. A distinction I drew in chapter 1 between the secular self and the moral self may be helpful here, as well as the other distinction between physical man and moral man. My identity as a physical, biological Being is made up of physical properties. My self-identity, my being self to my self, consists in my conscious thoughts and actions, my feelings and plans. My identity as a moral self, as a person, is a function of my acceptance of responsibility for my actions, perhaps also for some of my thoughts and intentions. The function of consciousness as an identifying or individuating agent is not limited to the person. As we have seen, it also identifies the soul-spirit as some man's soul-spirit. It also identifies some self as a particular self of some man or person. Consciousness is, we might say, an all-encompassing individuator. It individuates a person when consciousness is accompanied by a sense of responsibility, a recognition of the morality of our actions. The person becomes the locus of responsibility. The judgment to be made at the resurrection concerns the moral person, not the man per se.[10] Perhaps it would be better to say the judgment concerns the personhood of the man.[11]

This locution, "the personhood of the man", indicates that the person does not appear at the resurrection alone, as if the person could be disembodied. While person is characterized as a thinking, intelligent Being in 2.27.9, Locke also refers to person as a name or a term. He does not, I believe, speak of person as a real Being, as he does for the soul, but there may be no difference between a Being and a real Being. Nor does he locate the person on the chain of being. Nevertheless, both uses of 'Being' seem to have an ontological flavor, not just a linguistic sense. Still, it is clearly misleading to think of the person without the man, whether in this or the next life. As we have seen, man is also characterized as an intellectual, thinking, sensible Being, and man is located on the chain. But the man does not function in this life without a body, and Locke suggests that the man will have some bodily form at the resurrection. Nor can the man function in this life without a soul. We can say that body, man, and person form a unit, all three appear at the resurrection.

2.2. Sameness of Spirit

Locke refers to an enquiry into "What makes the same *Spirit, Man* or *Person*" (2.27.15), but I cannot find any place in the *Essay* where he explicates 'same spirit'. The sameness of spirit is clearly a function of consciousness, to the particular contents of the life of a man. Is it possible to separate or distinguish the thoughts that a man has from those of his soul? In individuating a soul by the particular conscious thoughts it has, have we at the same time individuated a man? Is the identity of a man the same as the identity of his soul? What are the marks of sameness of spirit? Locke uses the phrase 'same spirit' sparingly. The passage from *Essay* 2.27.14 cited above reads as follows: "Let any one reflect upon himself, and conclude, that he has in himself an immaterial Spirit, which is that which thinks in him, and in the constant change of his Body keeps him the same; and is that which he calls himself: Let him also suppose it to be the same Soul, that was in *Nestor* or *Thersites*, at the Siege of *Troy*". Here it is the sameness of soul, not same consciousness, that makes the same man. Notice the change from 'spirit' to 'soul'; they seem meant to be interchangeable. Section 29, the final section of that chapter, confidently remarks that "supposing a rational Spirit be the *Idea* of a *Man*, 'tis easie to know, what is the *same Man, viz.* the *same Spirit*, whether separate or in a Body will be the *same Man*". We would like to know what makes the same spirit, but Locke does not say, or perhaps he thinks he has given some clue in the following explication of 'same man'. In this passage he is clearly more concerned with the concept of same man. Three different ideas of a man are presented in this section, the first is the one just cited: man is a rational spirit. The second idea of man is "a rational Spirit vitally united to a Body of a certain conformation of Parts". So long as that spirit remains "in a fleeting successive Body", it will be the same man. The third idea of same man is close to the one he gave in 2.29.6, "the vital union of Parts in a certain shape". If we take the first definition of man to be 'rational spirit', then sameness of spirit determines the man, so long as it is the same spirit, so long as it continues to exist. On the second definition of section 29, sameness of man would be a combination of same spirit and same bodily parts. On the third definition, spirit or soul is no longer part of the notion of man. I suggested that Locke may have thought these examples contained some hint as to sameness of spirit, namely, continued existence, but that hardly seems clarifying in the absence of some account of the nature of the existence of spirits. So it seems to me the idea of same spirit continues to be left out of the account.

Chapter 27 begins the discussion of identity and diversity by listing three sorts of substances: God, finite intelligences, and bodies. Finite intelligences become finite spirits in his explication of sameness or identity. "Finite Spirits having had each its determinate time and place of beginning to exist, the relation to that time and place will always determine to each of them its Identity as long as it exists" (2.27.2).[12] There is no mention of consciousness as involved in its identity. The general principle for identity or sameness is given in the first section: "When therefore we demand, whether any thing be the same or no, it refers always to something that existed such a time in such a place, which 'twas certain, at that instant, was the same with it self and no other" (2.27.1). The discussion then proceeds to consider particles of matter (bodies) and "the Actions of finite Beings", the actions of those Beings, not the Beings themselves (2.27.2). Those actions are identified as motion and thought, the first the action of bodies, the second actions of finite Beings. The finite intelligences or spirits of the second kind of substances are responsible for thoughts. They are that which thinks in us. Thoughts occur successively, and each thought has "a different beginning of Existence" (2.27.2). Again, the general principle is "Existence it self . . . determines a Being of any sort [except God?] to a particular time and place" (2.27.3).[13] Locke goes on to discuss masses of matter, an oak tree, plants (§4), animals (§5) and man (§6). Then section 7 begins the discussion of the idea of identity or sameness by listing three referents of that idea: same substance, same man, and same person. The finite spirits mentioned in the previous sections are overlooked, and there is no discussion of same spirit.

Aside from the absence of any explication of the idea of same spirit, the difficulty of interpreting Locke is complicated by not knowing whether or when he is talking in his own voice. The chapter on identity and diversity raises all sorts of possibilities and puzzles about self and person identity. But Locke was insistent throughout those sections that personal identity resides in consciousness, not in immaterial spirit or soul. When he writes about a particular idea, e.g., the idea of a man, we cannot always determine when he is just reporting on how his contemporaries used that term, or when he is offering his analysis of that idea as information about the referent of that idea, information about man or about body. To make interpreting Locke even more difficult, we have to recognize that for him we are unable to discover the nature of man or of body, our only access is to the experiential features. Presumably the nature of spirits is no more accessible to experience than are bodies. Sometimes Locke draws out the implications or consequences of a particular idea. Thus, with the question about the talking parrot who was able to carry on a rational, coherent conversation, he remarks that what keeps the parrot from being considered a man is the absence of a proper shape. "For I presume 'tis not the *Idea* of a thinking or rational Being alone, that makes the *Idea* of a *Man* in most Peoples Sense; but of a Body so and so shaped joined to it" (2.27.8). Most people's idea may not be Locke's idea. He ends this passage by saying, with that idea of a man, the immaterial spirit goes to making the same man. So same man is linked with the thinking, immaterial spirit, as well as with a body of specific shape.[14]

These references to immaterial spirit are all in 2.27. The other chapter where that reference is found is 2.23, the discussion of substance. As we have seen, section 15 of that chapter describes the way we form the complex idea of an immaterial spirit "by the simple *Ideas* we have taken from those Operations of our own Minds, which we experience daily in our selves, as Thinking, Understanding, Willing, Knowing, and Power of beginning Motion" (2.23.15). Are all of these operations also ascribed to the soul-spirit? Distinguishing between spiritual and corporeal Beings, he says we know the latter by seeing and hearing. He does not say how we know spiritual Beings, but in this passage it is "the spiritual Being within" that we know: we know it "more certainly" than we do corporeal Beings external to us. We might say, we know it without observation. Locke is less specific: because we see and hear, and more generally think, we 'know' there is something in us that does the seeing, hearing, and thinking. Is this some kind of inference, perhaps an immediate inference? It sounds strange to say something in me, not me myself, does the seeing, hearing, and thinking. One assumption seems to be that seeing, hearing, thinking are spiritual, that is, mental, non-corporeal activities. From some similar actions, Descartes drew the conclusion that he was a thing that thinks, not that something in him was that thing. His conclusion may not be any sounder than Locke's. We may feel that Locke's claim here is a rather shaky knowledge claim, but what is important for Locke's ontology is the confirmation yet again that that ontology includes immaterial spirits, spiritual Beings. Locke was quick to remind us that we only know the sensible qualities of body and only the properties of thinking, willing, etc., of spirits, not the nature (inner constitution) of either (§17). The same description is given in section 22: "our *Idea* of our Soul, as an immaterial Spirit, is of a Substance that thinks, and has a power of exciting Motion in Body, by Will, or Thought". In section 31 he admits that "this Notion of immaterial Spirit may have, perhaps, some difficulties in it, not easie to be explained", but there is no reason to "deny, or doubt the existence of such Spirits".[15]

3. Immortality and Bodily Shape

No reason to doubt the existence of spirits, but we could wish for some elaboration, more detail on the spirits that inhabit our bodies and are vitally united to it. It is clear at least that to the four terms that run throughout 2.27 (man, self, person, agent) we need to add spirit. In my analysis in chapter 1 of those four terms, I tried to take man as the basic term. Man is the proprietor of his person; he is self to his self, and the agent of actions. Instrumental to man are the faculties, the passions, his abilities to reflect, to judge, to suspend judgment, and to exercise his will. The habit of writers then to assign specific tasks

Souls That Become Spirits 131

to these different components, e.g., to the mind or soul, should not lead us to view Locke's man as a spectator of that which thinks in him. That very phrase makes it sound as if the man does not think, has no control over his thoughts. A parallel could be seen in the mechanism of the body, the neurophysiological events in brain and nervous system which must function if we are to move our arms and legs. We might be tempted to say, we do not move our body, the physiology does. With his stress on immaterial principles and powers in the explanation of events, we can confidently say Locke would reject such a physicalist interpretation. Would he, in a kind of move, typical of Malebranche, embrace the notion that the soul does the thinking and moving, not the man? That is what he says in several passages, as we have seen. But is it what he meant?

He certainly seems to have subscribed to the doctrine of the separation of the soul from the body at death. The spirits that inhabit our bodies join the ranks of spirits on the chain and will, under certain conditions, enjoy eternal duration.[16] So despite the lack of any details on the sameness of spirit, we have to give the soul or spirit some special status within the group of four: man, self, person, and agent. The addition of spirit to that group is not just another term for soul, nor is it only what a man calls himself, although that aspect of a spirit is of great importance. The larger and more significant role of the spirits that inhabit our bodies is as a member of the ranks of spirits on the chain of being. Those spirits can ascend up the chain, although such a move up the ranks may depend upon the man having been a just man.[17] We might say man depends on the spirit in this life, but the spirit seems to depend upon the man for its status in the next life. In the absence of any details, we can only conjecture about the dependence. For example, does the distance the spirit goes up the chain vary with the degree of justness of the man?

In the absence of any analysis of same spirit, are we to understand that the spirits that inhabit our bodies are individuated by their attachments to specific bodies? More precisely, since the specific conscious thoughts and acts of thinking seem, in some passages, sufficient for the identity of a soul-spirit, what relation is there between the consciousness of the spirit and the body of the man? The body seems to be necessary for the identity of the man, at least of the physical man. Is it also necessary for moral man? Is it the man as agent that appears at the resurrection or his selfness and personhood, together with consciousness of his past actions? Locke was drawn into debate over the question about the body at the resurrection: must it be the same body? Not necessarily, Locke insisted, but he seems to have believed there would be some bodily form.[18] He was emphatic, however, that the shape of the human body has nothing to do with immortality. His spirited critique of the status of changelings insists that "the outward Shape and Appearance of a Man" is not designed for "an immortal future Being, after this Life" (4.4.15). Nor is human birth sufficient for a future life. He labels these two notions "Imaginations" that are "groundless and ridiculous". He carries on at some heated length:

> No one yet, that ever I heard of, how much soever immersed in Matter, allow'd that Excellency to any Figure of the gross sensible outward parts, as to affirm eternal Life due to it, or necessary consequence of it; or that any mass of Matter should, after its dissolution here, be again restored hereafter to an everlasting state of Sense, Perception, and Knowledge, only because it was molded into this or that Figure, and had such a particular frame of its visible parts.

This issue must have been of some importance for Locke, for he continues:

> This is to attribute more to the outside, than inside of Things; to place the Excellency of a Man, more in the external Shape of his Body, than internal Perfections of his Soul: which is but little better than to annex the great and inestimable advantage of Immortality and Life everlasting,

which he has above other material Beings, to annex it, I say, to the Cut of his Beard, or the Fashion of his Coat.

There is even more in this impassioned speech, but Locke's opinion is clear from these passages: bodily shape is irrelevant to immortality, even if there will be some shape in the next life, assuming that spiritual bodies will have a shape.[19] It is clear from these passages that sense, perception, and knowledge will be restored. Does that restoration require a body of some sort? Locke's comment in *Essay* 2.27.15 was that the person at the resurrection would be the same person, "though in a Body not exactly in make or parts the same which he had here". Just what those parts and make would be, he does not conjecture, so we cannot say what 'bodily' features are necessary for the restoration of sense, perception, and knowledge. In 4.4.15, it is a "mass of Matter" that is restored to "an everlasting state of Sense, Perception, and Knowledge", so in that late *Essay* section he was still thinking of a physical body.[20] The question of the exact nature of the body at the resurrection was, I suspect, of less concern for Locke than the faculties that are attached to that body. What was important for Locke was the restoration of those abilities to sense, perceive, and acquire knowledge, now a knowledge of quite a different sort from the limited knowledge acquired in the earthly life. What it is that is sensed, perceived, or known is unspecified.

I suggested in chapter 3 that while Locke's comments on his extravagant conjecture was that altered sense organs would be of no use for us in this life, nevertheless he seemed to find that possibility attractive. Just think, he seems to say, what wonderful knowledge about the inner constitution of matter such enhanced sense organs would yield. Perhaps this possibility is what will be realized in the next life: what he will be able to sense, perceive and know is, inter alia, the insensible corpuscles of bodies, their causal powers and qualities. It is tempting to suggest that this possibility of being able to penetrate beyond the senses, and to understand the structure and working of corpuscular mater was considered by Locke as one of the prime rewards and values of the bliss and happiness to be enjoyed by just men. The possession of such knowledge was at least part of "the great and inestimable advantage of immortality and Life everlasting".

Conclusion

What few details Locke offers about spirits indicate, I suspect, incomplete thoughts on these theological issues. These issues are related to or mirror some of the philosophical questions left incompletely analyzed in the *Essay*. There is a kind of tension between the notion of a fundamental constitution of man and the spirits that move the body and produce thoughts. This is a version of the mind-body or brain-mind problem which still plagues much of contemporary philosophy. If, as Locke insisted in a number of passages, immaterial forces are what cause the body to move, he would know that the body will not move unless specific physiological events occur in the body. Does spirit move the body by activating the physiology? The flow-from relation of the constitution of man is a causal relation, so where is there room for the man as agent to play a role (a question that Kant struggled to solve)?[21] If spirit does move the body, how is the man or person responsible for the actions? These are of course standard issues in philosophy. There are not many, if any, satisfactory resolutions to be found in the history of philosophy. Their appearance in Locke's *Essay* shifts them, as it were, up the chain of Being and lends them a theological flavor.

We might say that the theology of the *Essay* is contained in his account of the second sense of the notion of an intellectual world. The *Essay* is a bit short on details about that world, about the life of its inhabitants, the actions engaged in, what is done with that superior knowledge the spirits and the souls of just men possess. What we do have from his various remarks spread throughout the *Essay* is a belief in immortality that involves the soul, but where the soul may not be the most important item. At least for the judgment, it is the person and the consciousness of his past actions (all of them, now, I assume) that determine the nature of the judgment, good or bad. If, as some passages say, the soul is the man (or it is what a man considers to be himself) and if the soul is what thinks in a man and is the source of consciousness of the man (that which thinks is what is conscious), then we may have in Locke's account a single unit: the immortality of the soul is the immortality of the man. The secular unit of body, man, and person is transferred into the eschatological unit given eternal life.

Besides the important material on the souls of men that become spirits on the chain of being, the *Essay* gives us some fascinating hints, conjectures, suppositions and opinions about the spirits that dwell in that intellectual world. How firm a belief in such notions Locke held may not be clear, but from the extensive and repeated references, it seems safe to say he was expressing his own beliefs. As far as I can determine, the *Essay* is the main place, almost the only place, where he discusses the chain of being, angels and spirits. The few references in other books that I have cited confirm that the views in the *Essay* were anticipated in his other writings, even some of his earliest writings. But the details, in so far as there are any, are to be found in the work on the human understanding. The interesting question is why was this material on souls, spirits and angels included in a book devoted to the extent and limits of human knowledge? I think we can say that the *Essay* turns out to be a rather comprehensive account of Locke's thought on topics which he insists are beyond experience, perhaps also beyond conception and human understanding?

CHAPTER SIX

GENERAL CONCLUSION

Locke's two intellectual worlds span most of his interests. The world described in the final chapter of the *Essay* concerns the ordinary world, the material world in which we live. The three provinces identified in that chapter are a compendious way of organizing our knowledge and beliefs about the physical world, our perceptual acquaintance with the objects in our environment, as well as the actions performed by Locke's man, both cognitive and moral actions. The general methodology recommended for making discoveries about objects is experience and observation, supplemented by clarification of important ideas and words so that ambiguities can be avoided and our language for talking and communicating about objects and human actions can be made more precise. Locke believed we have a duty and an obligation to employ our faculties in the discovery of truth and to extend our knowledge. But that injunction goes along with a healthy recognition of the limits of human understanding. Beyond the reach of understanding, belief is to be governed by rationality and intelligibility, and what is consistent with our experience.

These careful guides for knowledge, truth, and belief do not rule out conjectures, suppositions, guesses, possibilities about aspects of the physical world beyond our experience, such as the corpuscular theory of matter, or the possibility of thought added to organized matter by God. The references to an underlying or fundamental constitution of objects and of man, including the inner constitution of children, a constitution from which flows the observed properties of objects and the active faculties of man, represent other departures from the method of experience and observation. Those conjectures and suppositions are part of the intellectual world of *Essay* 4.21.

For those who still cling to labeling Locke 'empiricist' (of whom there are fewer today), it may take some getting used to hearing Locke define natural philosophy as what we might term a 'speculative science', to say nothing about his application of that science to spirits. He does not use the term 'science' to describe natural philosophy; he may have wanted to reserve that term for the experimental science he so carefully described and recommended for the study of physical nature and, in some sense, for the study of human understanding and the cognitive faculties. The term 'science' is also applied to the possibility of an a priori science of nature, a deduction from the inner constitution of bodies. This is a possibility not open to humans. From what he says in a number of places, God, Angels and some Spirits have this sort of knowledge of bodies and, I think, of humans because of their special powerful faculties. We could speak of three methods to science, using 'science' in the generic sense of systematic knowledge: the method of experience and observation, the method of deduction from inner constitution, and the direct access to inner constitutions had by God, Angels and Spirits. The speculations and conjectures of natural philosophy would then be a fourth method. Of these four methods, only the first and fourth are possible for us. I suggested earlier that the experimental method is employed by scientists such as Boyle and Sydenham. It may be that Locke's account of the understanding and the mind's various modes of operation is in a way an application of the experimental method to those areas, but the full application of that method to those areas was done by Hume who developed the experimental method for the science of man or the moral sciences. Just how we are to characterize those important parts of the *Es-*

say that analyze the understanding and the other faculties may not be entirely clear or unequivocal. It is easier for us to say that Locke is doing natural philosophy in the *Essay*, a method he applies to man and to spirits. Perhaps we should say that when dealing with the extent and limits of human understanding, he employs both the method of experience and observation and the method of speculation and conjecture: experimental science and natural philosophy.

There is a very interesting passage in the early *Essays on the Law of Nature* which may be seen as yet another method to science (or knowledge) or at least as casting some methodological light on what Locke was doing in the *Essay*. The topic of lecture 4 in the *Essays* was the role of reason in the knowledge of natural law. For Locke, reason was always an important faculty, rationality was, as we have seen, one of the defining properties of man. There was a tradition behind Locke of referring to the light of reason or the light of nature. Innatists claimed this was a gift from God implanted in the soul at birth. That light served as a source of knowledge of moral laws. Locke, of course, strongly rejected the claim of innatists, but in these early *Essays* he retains the light of nature while redefining it. He explains in lecture 2: "by saying that something can be known by the light of nature, we mean nothing else but that there is some sort of truth to the knowledge of which a man can attain by himself and without the help of another, if he makes proper use of the faculties he is endowed with by nature" (p. 123). Having rejected the claim that the light of nature is a moral principle "written in our minds by nature", he characterizes it as reason working with sense experience (p. 147). He goes on to make the disturbing claim (disturbing to the innatists and traditionalists) that "these two faculties appear to teach and educate the minds of men and to provide what is characteristic of the light of nature", and here he seems to make a more general claim than just a claim about moral principles, "that things otherwise wholly unknown and hidden in darkness should be able to come before the mind and be known and as it were looked into" (p. 147).

If reason and sense work properly together, "there is nothing so obscure, so concealed, so removed from any meaning that the mind, capable of everything, could not apprehend it by reflection and reasoning" (p. 147). It would be interesting to have him expand on this confident statement about the mind's ability to discover what is concealed and to give meaning to what is "removed from any meaning". In this passage, it is reflection, not sense, that works with reason, but he does not say how reflection works to give meaning to what seemed without meaning. It is just these references to things hidden and unknown, and to the obscure and concealed that, read against the background of his conjectures and guesses about spirits, catches my attention. Even more attention-grabbing is a remark a few sentences after those I have just cited. "And if there are things obscure, sublime, and noble, which even reason itself may marvel at and bring forth and proclaim as a discovery, yet, if you would run through each single speculative science, there is none in which something is not always presupposed and taken for granted and derived from the senses by way of borrowing" (p. 151).[1] Except for that last phrase about the senses, this remark might easily be applied to his account of spirits. He adds an intriguing comment relative to the speculative science of the *Essay:* "Every concept about the mind as well about the body always arises out of some pre-existing material, and reason proceeds in the same manner in the moral and practical sciences also and demands to be allowed this material".

Whether we can identify the 'pre-existing material' about the mind or soul on which his account rests or what it presupposes, I am not sure. Nor would it be easy to find some presuppositions for his account of the chain of being or spirits, especially for the spirits that inhabit our bodies. The questions I have raised about the meaningfulness of some of his references, such as the happiness of God and angels, the nature of the body at the resurrection, the many examples of what is and is not conceivable may be partially resolved by recognizing that involved in Locke's account are things obscure, hidden, and even noble and beautiful. One conclusion from these passages in the early

Essays that we can draw is that even as early as 1643–44 when those lectures were composed, Locke did not shy away from things hidden and removed from meaning. Of course, in the *Essays* he tried to find a basis in sense experience for the materials from which reflection and reason drew conclusions. The later *Essay concerning Human Understanding* was in some ways even bolder in its use of items that go beyond experience, the many creatures, Beings and spirits that inhabit the different mansions of the universe, the second intellectual world in particular. These departures from experience may well have been driven by theological concerns.

The more fascinating of the two intellectual worlds in Locke's *Essay* is that beautiful, perfect domain of God, Angels and Spirits. Here, supposition, guesses, and conjectures run free, with little to guide the content save some biblical references, an accepted notion of a chain of being, and probably some other unnamed writers who 'tell' us about spirits. In chapter 4 we saw Locke's rather detailed account of how we can enlarge our ideas of some of the properties of spirits. His claim was that such ideas are combinations of simple ideas. When it comes to conjecture, guessing and supposing, would he make the same claim? If conjectures and guesses are to be intelligible, they may involve ideas or, a term he sometimes uses instead, 'notions', ideas and notions that are functions of simple ideas. There is a remark at the close of that extravagant conjecture about the possibility that spirits can assume bodies and adapt their sense organs to objects which bears on this topic. Admitting that God could "frame Creatures with a thousand other Faculties, and ways of perceiving things without them, than what we have", he says firmly that "our Thoughts can go no farther than our own, so impossible it is for us to enlarge our very Guesses, beyond the *Ideas* received from our own Sensation and Reflection" (2.23.13). Locke certainly made an effort, with those several examples of enlarging ideas, to limit the ideas of spirits in this way. Whether we find him entirely successful in this effort, we need to recognize the fact that his program of deriving all ideas from sensation and reflection was applied in this area as well. It may be useful to remind ourselves of a caution he offers in the introduction to the *Essay:*

> If by this Enquiry into the Nature of the Understanding, I can discover the Powers thereof; *how far* they reach; to what things they are in any Degree proportionate; and where they fail us, I suppose it may be of use, to prevail with the busy Mind of Man, to be more cautious in meddling with things exceeding its Comprehension; to stop, when it is at the utmost Extent of its Tether; and to sit down in a quiet Ignorance of those Things, which, upon Examination, are found to be beyond the reach of our Capacities (1.1.4).

He urges us not to be

> so forward, out of an Affectation of an universal Knowledge, to raise Questions, and perplex our selves and others with Disputes about Things, to which our Understandings are not suited; and of which we cannot frame in our Minds any clear or distinct Perceptions, or whereof (as it has perhaps too often happen'd) we have not any Notions at all.

I have suggested that all that he says about angels and spirits may not be supported by clear or distinct perceptions, but that he had 'notions' about the universe and its various inhabitants, especially those Beings in the second intellectual world, is very clear from the *Essay.*

It may be a bit difficult to gauge the strength of Locke's belief in the existence and nature of those spirits, but the sheer number of references to spirits and the many ways in which their nature, faculties and operations help him explain some of the main notions of the *Essay* indicates the importance spirits had for him, an importance highlighted by his clear identification of the human soul as one of the spirits on the chain of being. Moreover, the sharp difference in attitude towards spirits and their role in the *Essay* from the accounts found in Burthogge and Bekker give special significance to Locke's account embedded in a major work on human understanding.

However reluctant some readers may be to recognize the role of spirits in Locke's thought, there can be no doubt about his belief in immortality, the Judgment Day, and the infinite happiness and bliss to be acquired by just men.[2] What Locke tries to do on those topics is to identify the locus of responsibility for human actions, to determine the basis on which the judgment at the resurrection will be made. That is one important reason for his distinction between man and person, and also for his linking consciousness with the actions done by persons. Consciousness of our actions enables us to take responsibility for them.

To have worked out the details of human responsibility still does not deal with another ingredient in the Christian doctrine, the human soul. Here, Locke's account of separate spirits comes together with his finding a role for the soul at the resurrection. The soul's role at the resurrection is somewhat limited or compromised by the key role of the person. There seems to be a tension (perhaps even a rivalry) in his account between the immortal soul and the person. The soul seems to be downgraded. There may be a question as to how far he departs from the Christian doctrine of the soul in his giving a first-order preference to the person (with the consciousness of the actions of the man) at the resurrection. On the other hand, the person is not described as a real Being, nor does the person have a place on the chain of being. The soul may acquire importance by being one of the spirits on the chain, the one in fact that inhabits our bodies. That expression, 'that inhabits our bodies', makes the soul sound like a foreign entity attached, in some way, to the man. To say the soul or spirit is that which thinks in us reinforces this misleading notion. A dual task confronts Locke (or confronts us when we try to understand him): (a) to find a role for the soul at the resurrection and (b) to integrate the soul into that complex of man, self and person. Locke accomplished neither of these tasks. At least, there is no clearcut account of either in the *Essay*, only a few hints, as we have seen.

Locke's man is a thinking, rational Being but also a corporeal, biological organism. Thinking, perceiving and cognitive actions are not performed by the body, although the body (certainly the brain) is involved in and plays a supporting role in the thinking and perceiving. Consciousness in general is more than physiology. How is that 'more' to be characterized? As we have seen, Locke likes to say there is something in us that thinks, i.e., the soul or mind or spirit. The 'in' of this phrase does not mean that the mind, soul or spirit is located physically in the body or brain, although he does work with a concept of place or location that applies to the non-corporeal functions of the man. In part, this concept of place or location captures the fact that we do not think apart from our bodies. To say, as he does, that the soul (that which thinks in us) moves from London to Oxford when the man makes that journey, is simply a recognition of the vital union between the body and the thinking that we engage in. Thought, we might say, rides on the back of our neurophysiology, but this metaphor needs to be explicated. Some might say thought is an emergent or a supervenient phenomenon, this being another way to stress the ontological difference between that phenomenon and the physical and neurological actions of the body. Locke's way of catching this difference is to say the soul is a real Being, just as the body is a real Being.

So I think we must recognize that Locke's concept of man, of a finite human being, did not consider man to be fragmented into parts, at least not into unrelated parts. His notion of a vital union of physical and mental clearly was his way of expressing an organic unit. There are various components of this unit, the physical and psychological, features vitally necessary for action: perception and thought; the cognitive and affective features; the functions of reasoning, judging, choosing, deliberating; and the power of thinking and acting. Throughout the *Essay* he alternates between tracing some of these actions and faculties to the mind or to the soul, and occasionally to the spirit. Just as we might distinguish the secular self from the moral self, or rational from moral man, we might interpret his use of mind, soul and spirit as three aspects of (or three names for) the non-physical active ingredients of man. 'Mind' could be seen as the secular name, 'soul' as the religious name in this life, and 'spirit' as the theological name for the next life.

Just as the person emerges from the man, so the theological importance of the soul arises from and is closely related to the moral self and its concern for eternal happiness. Happiness, both temporal and eternal, was of great significance for Locke. Preparation in this life for the happiness (and the avoidance of misery) in the next was an urgent concern. On more than one occasion, he urges all men, not just the few, to focus on this ultimate goal. Here are three examples.

(1) Of the Conduct of the Understanding. In section 7, Locke points out the usefulness of mathematics as a model of reasoning, but he recognizes that not everyone has the time or the skill to follow mathematical demonstrations. "Knowledge and Science in general, is the business only of those who are at Ease and Leisure" (p. 35). Those who have what he labels "particular Callings" for the "support of Life" have, as I noted earlier a concern for a future life. That concern causes those persons to think about religion, where it is very important "to understand and reason right". The words and language of religion as well as its general notions need to be understood. "The one Day of seven, besides other Days of Rest, allows in the Christian World time enough for this (had they no other idle Hours) if they would but make use of these vacancies from their daily Labour, and apply themselves to an improvement of Knowledge, with as much diligence as they often do to a great many other things that are useless" (pp. 35–36). The nature of the minds of ordinary men, men with daily jobs to perform, is the same as those who have the leisure to master science and mathematics. There are "instances of very mean [ordinary, working] people, who have raised their Minds to a great Sense and Understanding of Religion. And though these have not been so frequent as could be wished, yet they are enough to clear that Condition of Life from a necessity of gross ignorance, and to shew that more might be brought to be rational Crea-

tures and Christians" (p. 36). Even if we believe that "the meaner sort of People must give themselves up to a brutish Stupidity in the things of their nearest Concernments, which I see no reason for, this excuses not those of a freer Fortune and Education" to neglect their understanding and fail to use their faculties carefully (p. 37).

In these pages, we have a rationale for the enterprise Locke undertook in his *Essay*. We also find a firm stress on the importance of those greater concerns, a reference to the judgment in the next life and the happiness or misery waiting for us there.

(2) The Reasonableness of Christianity. In a well-known passage, Locke remarks on the difficulty of "unassisted Reason, to establish Morality" (p. 148). It is, he says, "at least a surer and shorter way, to the Apprehensions of the vulgar, and mass of Mankind, that one manifestly sent from God, and coming with visible Authority from him, should as a King and Lawmaker tell them their Duties". The trains of reasoning required to reach conclusions about morality and religion are beyond the "greatest part of Mankind [who] have neither leisure to weigh; nor, for want of Education and Use, skill to judge of" the trains of reasoning in determining their duty (cf. pp. 153–54). The 'trains of reasoning' probably reflects his suggestion in the *Essay* that a demonstrative morality could be constructed, deriving moral rules by reason. His early *Essays on the Law of Nature* claimed that reason together with sense-perception could discover the law of nature (pp. 147–59). In the passage from *Reasonableness* he cites other causes preventing many from knowing moral laws: "Men's Necessities, Passions, Vices, and mistaken Interests" that stand in the way of a knowledge of morality (p. 149).

(3) An Essay concerning Human Understanding. The penultimate chapter of this work explores the reasons and causes for some men giving "their Assents contrary to Probability" (4.20.1). He offers four reasons for wrong assent, the first being the want of proofs, proofs that already exist and are available

for anyone to consider and understand. Most men "have not the Convenience, or Opportunity to make Experiments and Observations themselves" which would support some proposition (4.20.2). This is the condition of "the greatest part of Mankind, who are given up to Labour, and enslaved to the Necessity of their mean Condition; whose Lives are worn out, only in the Provisions for Living". As with the passages from the *Conduct* and the *Reasonableness,* he spells out in even more striking terms the way in which the struggle for living prevents the bulk of mankind from acquiring first hand the time and abilities necessary for acquiring knowledge, especially a knowledge of their duty.

> These Men's Opportunity of Knowledge and Enquiry, are commonly as narrow as their Fortunes; and their Understandings are but little instructed, when their whole Time and Pains is laid out, to still the Croaking of their own Bellies, or the Cries of their Children. 'Tis not to be expected, that a Man, who drudges on, all his Life, in a laborious Trade, should be more knowing in the variety of Things done in the World, than a Pack-horse, who is driven constantly forwards and backwards, in a narrow Lane, and dirty Road, only to Market, should be skilled in the Geography of the Country. Nor is it at all more possible, that he who wants Leisure, Books, and Languages, and the Opportunity of Conversing with variety of Men, should be in a Condition to collect those Testimonies and Observations, which are in Being, and are necessary to make out many, nay most of the Propositions, that, in the Societies of Men, are judged of the greatest Moment. (4.20.2)

Does this mean that "the greatest part of Mankind, by the necessity of their Condition, [are] subjected to unavoidable Ignorance in those Things, which are of greatest Importance to them"? (4.20.3). Just what are those things of greatest importance is revealed in the next two sentences: "Have the Bulk of Mankind no other Guide, but Accident, and blind Chance, to conduct them to their Happiness, or Misery? Are the current Opinions, and licensed Guides of every Country sufficient Evidence and Security to every Man, to venture his greatest Concernments on; nay, his everlasting Happiness, or Misery?" (4.20.3). His answer to this question is hopeful: "No Man is so wholly taken up with the Attendance on the Means of Living, as to have no spare Time at all to think of his Soul, and inform himself in Matters of Religion".

These three excerpts from three different books attest to the importance Locke placed on morality and the concerns for happiness or misery in the next life. We might think it quite proper for such sentiments to be part of his *Reasonableness,* but even in the two works on human understanding, the urgency surfaces for reminding all men, all human beings, of that fateful day of judgment. In Locke's mind there is a close connection between the pursuit of knowledge by proper methods and the preparation for the life to come. Thus, it is no accident that he gives so much attention in the *Essay* to the second intellectual world, the domain of God, Angels and Spirits. The two intellectual worlds of John Locke are closely linked.

There is another linkage that needs some brief attention: the relation between accounts in Locke's *Essay* and *Reasonableness* concerning resurrection and eternal life. We have seen passages in the latter that refer to happiness and immortality, to two kinds of bodies (physical and spiritual), at least one reference to the intellectual world, another to degrees of spirits, quite a few to eternal life. There are also several mentions of angels, some of devils, but no reference to a chain of Being. These references provide some continuity between the two books. I have characterized the second intellectual world of the *Essay* as the domain of God, Angels and Spirits. This description fits the account in that work. We might think of that account as the secular or ontological version of what the *Reasonableness* refers to as the 'Kingdom of God', a theological version of the second intellectual world of the *Essay*. To be more precise, my suggested identification of the second intellectual world with the Kingdom of God may not be quite correct. There are two other kingdoms mentioned in Locke's explication of New Testament accounts of Jesus as the Messiah. Besides the Kingdom of God, there is the Kingdom of Heaven and, most importantly, the Kingdom of the Messiah. Locke explains that John the Baptist's "Repent, for the Kingdom of Heaven is at Hand" in Matthew 3:1.2 was "a declaration of the Coming of the Messiah; the Kingdom of Heaven and the Kingdom of God being the same" (p. 35). He goes on to say both Kingdoms signify "the Kingdom of the Messiah". Without getting into the subtleties of these theological concepts, it might perhaps be better to say that the second intellectual world of the *Essay* includes all three Kingdoms.[3]

Another way to characterize the relation between these two books is to view the *Essay* account as drawing out some of the epistemological and ontological implications of the concepts of the Kingdom of God, the Fall, and resurrection. The first chapter of the *Reasonableness* opens with Locke's interpretation of Adam's Fall. A proper interpretation of that Fall will, Locke suggests, help us understand "what we are returned to by Jesus Christ" (p. 5). What Adam lost was "Paradise, wherein was Tranquility and the Tree of Life, i.e. he lost Bliss and Immortality" (pp. 6, 9), an "Immortality and bliss [that] belongs to the Righteous" (p. 13). So Paradise was "a State of Immortality, of Life without end". Thus, the life "which Jesus Christ restores to all men [all just men?] is that Life which they receive at the Resurrection" (p. 12). What he is doing in the *Essay* is filling in some of the details of those theological notions: details of the way the moral person fits into that structure, where the soul finds a place in the resurrection among the other spirits, and the future state of just men. In a way, these components of the *Essay* humanize the stark theological doctrines of the Fall and future rewards and punishment. The metaphor of the chain of being furnishes Locke with one intelligible explanation of resurrection, a move up that chain into the second intellectual world, God's Kingdom. That metaphoric move made by the soul as a real Being translates into the soul's acquiring more reality and new relations. As that which thinks in us in this life, the soul's role in the next is not all that clear, but the fact that it takes its place among other immaterial spirits must give it some importance. The stress in the *Essay* was on the moral person, the Being who is to be judged on that Great Day.

As we have seen, the chain of being plays an important and pervasive role in Locke's account of the different creatures, Beings, and spirits that inhabit the various mansions of the universe. I am assuming that the second intellectual world does belong to some part of the universe, perhaps the universe in its broadest sense. But, as I have just remarked, the chain of being is a metaphor that captures, or enables Locke to subscribe to the notion of degrees of reality, to degrees of perfection, greater knowledge and happiness, at least for intelligent Beings. I commented much earlier on the developmental concepts he works with: development from infant to child to adult; from physical man to moral man and person; from finite and limited to infinite and eternal. Higher and lower on the chain captures some of these developments. The metaphor of the chain or scale with the upward and downward directions, its possibilities of ascent and descent, are significant for Locke's man, oriented as he wished him to be towards the ascent, with the terminus in the domain of God, Angels and Spirits.

Does the chain of being require or assume differences of kind, of species? We have found Locke referring to species of angels, but he has always been taken to deny human species of a fixed kind. There are at least two clear kind-differences, the one between man and animals and the other between man and angels and other spirits. There may be no differences of kind between humans, but there are some differences between humans and other intelligent Beings who probably have different faculties from humans. Locke speaks at one point of man being the lowest of intelligent Beings. Whether 'lowest' implies a kind-difference may be debatable. He says there are no chasms or gaps in the chain, but there is one fundamental gap at least, that between man and angels and spirits. Perhaps even that gap is bridged by the soul-spirit; men, just men are able to jump the gap with the help of the soul-spirit. Nevertheless, it is probably correct to say that the metaphor of the chain does not sanction kind-differences among that group of intelligent Beings we recognize as humans. I have suggested that the species differences made by scientists today on the basis of genetic and molecular differences are similar to Locke's fundamental constitution of man.

That fundamental constitution on which observed properties and functions depend is similar to the coded information in the genome. We are told that humans share large portions of their genome structure with mice and even plants, so here we may have anther example of that continuity in nature Locke spoke of in that striking passage of *Essay* 4.6.11. So if the scale or chain of being is taken to involve the notion of species, Locke's use of it may not support that notion. What is important about his use of that metaphor is the way in which it enables him to map the progress of man from this life to the next, the attractive prospect of perfection in knowledge and happiness and the many Beings that fill the universe.

The theological aspects of the *Essay* are by no means the central features of that work, but the ease with which the talk of Angels, Spirits and the second intellectual world are integrated into the *Essay* confirms the importance for Locke of the doctrines of his *Reasonableness*. Recognizing all these fascinating features of the *Essay* may also reveal the continuity of his thought over several of his books. It would be misleading to say the second beautiful intellectual world of the *Essay* is more important for him than the first, the world explored so carefully there. But we should recognize both components of his thought as central to his thinking.

The critics of the *Essay* in Locke's lifetime, and there were many, found fault with some of his assertions and doctrines. They saw these features of the *Essay* as threats to religion, undermining Christian doctrine. As my analysis in the previous chapters has shown, there is a clear, firm commitment in that work to the doctrines of resurrection of the dead, the immortality of the soul, the judgment of the just and the wicked, God as the creator of all creatures and Beings, the importance of virtue based on God's laws, and the existence of angels and separate spirits. All of these were integrated into a work on the human understanding, knowledge, and belief. Those religious aspects run as a kind of subplot through the *Essay*. It may be difficult for us to appreciate how all of those religious-oriented features could have been missed or misread. The answer lies in the alternative ontology and epistemology accepted, mostly uncritically, by those theologians who were disturbed by the *Essay*. A belief in real essences of a fixed kind, a belief in mind and body as two distinct substances fundamentally different, the immateriality of the soul as a necessary condition for immortality, and for some, the resurrection of man with the same body: these were the doctrines of most of Locke's contemporaries.

How many of those contemporary critics had a belief in angels and separate spirits, I do not know, but I rather think that was not a widely held notion among the divines who attacked Locke, or even among those who defended him. Apparently those early critics who rejected the *Essay* because of its denial of innate ideas did accept and value the existence of spirits. What they thought the connection was between innate ideas and the idea of spirits is far from clear. Nevertheless, had they read the *Essay* through before forming their judgment, as Locke advised, they would have discovered the many uses of spirits throughout the *Essay*, the several suggestions about their nature, faculties, and operations, and (most significant of all) his identification of the human soul as one of those spirits.

There were a number of different features of Locke's *Essay* that lead readers to take alarm and attack its doctrines without appreciating the extent to which Locke endorsed and used fundamental Christian beliefs in that work. One cause for the failure of his critics to appreciate the theology of the *Essay* was, I suspect, the novelty of his approach to the religious and moral values he accepted—not the novelty of the way of ideas so much as his presentation of man as composed of parts, especially parts that were vitally united to the body. The notion of a vital union of bodily and non-bodily parts, a notion not explicated by Locke, may have added to the suspicion of materialism in the *Essay*. Some of the parts or components in his account of man seem to be in competition with each other. Locke's division of tasks among the components could have misled or mystified some readers. Especially his assigning priority to the person at the resurrection, rather than to the soul, may have blinded some of his readers to the fact that the reason for the prominence of the person was that it enabled him to stress the importance of virtue and our acceptance of responsibility for our actions. While the soul is that which thinks and moves the body, the locus of responsibility and the agent of action (not the motion of the body in action) is the person. But since the soul is that which thinks, presumably it is also the source of the consciousness, which plays such a crucial role in personal identity; in this way, the soul is intimately involved in, as it were, creating the person. In the end, it is a single unit, perhaps minus the earthly body and that vital union with such a body, that moves up the chain and awaits judgment.

The *Essay* portrays man as firmly rooted in the physical world, the world of everyday life and the world of science. Human action takes place in that world but the very nature of action as intentional, governed by rules and accepted practices, introduces non-physical features into that world. Immateriality may not be necessary for immortality, as Locke argued (for reasons not entirely clear), but immaterial forces are required as explanatory principles, and the immaterial soul is, in Locke's account, firmly at work in human action. Man, a human Being, contains in one unit physical and immaterial forces. The great work on human understanding locates humans in the universe at large, among the myriads of Beings that inhabit other portions of the universe, and the soul-spirit that is housed in the body contains the potential for each human to join the ranks of angels and separate spirits in the second intellectual world, the Kingdom of Heaven. Such are the surprising, somewhat overlooked doctrines of that epistemological work.

NOTES

Introduction

1. In that book, I made a suggestion of the possible identity of some of those who condemned the *Essay* for its rejection of innate ideas, but whether those same writers defended the existence or idea of spirits, I do not know. At this distance from my earlier research, I no longer can retrieve any memory of this suggestion, or of any comments by seventeenth-century writers about the connection between innate ideas and the notion or proof of spirits. If by 'spirits' the reference is to the soul as a spirit, perhaps the point is that a soul is required as the receptacle of innate ideas, so without innate ideas, there would be no soul. In either case of spirits as souls or as separate Beings, the *Essay* contains Locke's acceptance of both. There is a research project here for some younger scholar who might go back and examine the writing before and contemporary with Locke on the topic of spirits and innate ideas.
2. In an interesting section of the 'Conduct of the Understanding' in which Locke is urging us to form our opinions only on the basis of evidence, he remarks: "I do not expect that by this way the Assent should in every one be proportion'd to the Grounds and Clearness wherewith every Truth is capable to be made out, or that Men should be perfectly kept from Error: That is more than humane Nature can by any means be advanc'd to; I am at no such unattainable Privilege" (§33). See also *Reasonableness*, pp. 154, 161–62.
3. Many of these same terms occur, not surprisingly, in Locke's *Two Treatises of Government*, 'human nature' and 'human life' in particular but also 'human affairs', 'human action', 'human laws', 'human frailty'.

The occurrence of these terms and phrases in both *Two Treatises* and the *Essay* might be seen as a mark of continuity between the two books.
4. Etienne Balibar: *Identité et différence. L'invention de la conscience*, p. 10. Balibar also points out that the long chapter on power and liberty, chapter 21, is in effect another treatise.

1. Locke's Man

1. In this chapter I do not discuss Kant's distinction. I mean only to remind us of the similarities between Kant and Locke on this topic. For some discussion of the similarities, see my *Realism and Appearances*, pp.45–56.
2. *Locke: His Philosophical Thought* (Oxford: Oxford University Press, 1999), p. 108.
3. Ibid., p. 101.
4. "Thus Locke's theory of personal identity is clearly consistent with substance materialism" (ibid. p. 107). The denial of immaterial substance is not the denial of immaterial, non-corporeal properties. Jolley does not seem to allow for property dualism.
5. For the explanation of hands feeling hot and cold in the same water, see *Essay*, 2.8.21. Also, see 2.27.13 where Locke raised the question of the connection of thought to "a System of fleeting Animal Spirits". See also 2.27.27. References to the *Essay concerning Human Understanding* are given in this way, the numbers referring to book, chapter, and section. Sometimes, the reference will be just to the numbers. In the *Education*, Locke urges parents and tutors to keep "Children from frights of all kinds; when they are young". The "habitual motion of the Animal Spirits, introduced by the first strong Impressions", may alter later behavior (§115). Section 167 in that work suggests that the difficulty children have holding their attention on a topic may be due to "the temper of their Brains, or the quickness or interruption of their Animal Spirits" (§167).
6. *Essay*, 2.27.15.
7. Ibid., 2.27.6. See also §8.
8. Ibid., 3.11.16. Early in the *Essay*, Locke describes "the whole Man" as consisting of "Mind as well as Body" (2.1.11).
9. *Essay*, 2.21.10.
10. This section (2.21.19) begins with saying some actual thought "may be the occasion of Volition, or exercising the power a Man has to chuse". The "choice of the Mind, [may be] the cause of actual thinking on this or that thing". In a similar way, "the actual singing of such a Tune, may be the occasion of dancing such a Dance, and the actual

dancing of such a Dance, [may be] the occasion of singing such a Tune". Does the term 'occasion' indicate Locke's attempt to avoid the use of 'cause'? Is choosing a power but one that does not cause the volition; is singing a power but one that does not cause the dance?

11. On thinking as a power, see 2.1.10: "We know certainly by Experience, that we sometimes think, and thence draw this infallible Consequence, That there is something in us, that has a Power to think".

12. Locke's "Conduct of the Understanding" opens with the observation: "for though we distinguish the Faculties of the Mind, and give the supreme Command to the Will, as to an Agent; yet the truth is, the Man which is the Agent determines himself to this or that Voluntary Action, upon some precedent Knowledge, or appearance of Knowledge in the Understanding" (§1).

13. For a summary statement of the pervasive role of powers in the physical world, see 3.2.2 and 3.2.3. There Locke talks of 'natural substances'. Most of the long chapter on power is devoted to the powers we have as agents.

14. E. J. Lowe, *Subjects of Experience* (Cambridge University Press, 1996), pp. 32–35. Marc Parmentier has suggested that the concept of person is a new category for Locke. The traditional doctrine of substance identified two kinds, material and immaterial. But humans, individual men embody both material and immaterial properties, extension and thought, so they do not fit into either one of the traditional categories. Parmentier refers to "une localisation concomitante des esprits et des corps". Following his remark, we might suggest that extension and thought are properties of the person, the person, we might say, plays the role of substance. Marc Parmentier, *Introduction à l'Essai sur l'entendement humain de Locke*, p. 183; see also pp. 271, 273.

15. For a useful discussion of the various locutions with the term 'self' in combination with other terms, see Balibar, *Identité et différence*, glossary entry for 'self'.

16. In chapter 5, I discuss some passages in which the same consciousness is said to make the same man.

17. Does Locke mean to include the possibility of immaterial substances being part of the production? He never ruled out such substances, even though they seem to play no role in personal identity. But if they are included in the production of actions, they may have a role to play. If the soul is an immaterial substance, then, as we will see later, it may not contribute to personal identity, although it is an important ingredient in the complex of man, self, and person. In fact, whether the soul is a substance or not, it is important in Locke's full account of man.

18. See also 2.21.50 (playing the fool can "draw Shame and Misery upon a Man's self"); 3.3.9 (we can consider "a Man's self"); and 4.11.2 (we

can only be certain of the existence of God and of "a Man's self"). This phrase is also found in Locke's *Education*, §175. The definition E. J. Lowe offered recently is of some interest in relation to Locke. "By a self, then, I mean a possible object of first-person reference and subject of first-person thoughts: a being which can think that it itself is thus and so and can identify itself as the unique subject of certain thoughts and experiences and as the unique agent of certain actions" (*Subjects*, p. 5). Notice Lowe's use of the word 'being'. He does not explain what 'a being' is. As did Locke also, that word is used in a neutral way, leaving open the ontological question of the status of 'a being'.

19. This is an odd remark. The finger would be the person if the consciousness goes along with it. Can we say, then, that the finger or my body is my self, so long as they are accompanied by my consciousness?

20. Locke makes liberal use of the term 'name' throughout the *Essay*. For example, to cite just a few: equality (1.2.16), atheist and sceptical (1.3.25), virtue (1.3.17), fire (1.4.11), cube and globe (2.9.8), husband (2.25.1), cause (2.26.1).

21. Cf. *Education*, §120: "When any new thing comes in their way, Children usually ask, the common Question of a Stranger: What is it? Whereby they ordinarily mean nothing but the Name; and therefore to tell them how it is call'd, is usually the proper Answer to that Demand".

22. This way of characterizing the difference in consciousness is suggested to me by a remark Parmentier makes late in his book: "Pour définir un sujet moral la *consciousness* ne doit cependant pas être seulement une conscience cognitive mais ouvrir un champ d'"intéressement' (*concernment*)" (p. 283). Parmentier's analysis of Locke's account of personal identity is an important contribution to that topic, it is an example of renewed interest in Locke by French scholars. Another more important study of this topic is Etienne Balibar's French translation, commentary, notes, and detailed glossary of *Essay* 2.27 (on personal identity): *Identité et différence. l'invention de la conscience* (1998). See my review in the *British Journal for the History of Philosophy* 10, no. 2 (June 2002): 310–12.

23. The role of concern in his account of personal identity is announced as early as 2.1.11: "For if we take wholly away all Consciousness of our Actions and Sensations, especially of Pleasure and Pain, and the concernment that accompanies it, it will be hard to know wherein to place personal Identity". The same section speaks several times of concern for "Happiness, or Misery" when dealing with the question of whether the waking Socrates is the same as the sleeping Socrates. See also 2.1.12.

24. If I appropriate some action by being conscious of it, that is sufficient

to count as my action. As odd or counter-intuitive as this remark may seem, it does reveal the importance of appropriation for Locke, as well as the weight he places on consciousness. There is an interesting reversal here of the situation of the man who while drunk commits some action but does not remember the action and hence does not appropriate it. In that case, we want to say the man did the action. In the case of a man who is conscious of actions as his that were committed a thousand years ago, we want to say that is impossible. Perhaps this case is no more strange than that of the consciousness that goes with the cut-off finger. Again consciousness, appropriation, is given great importance.

25. That the definition of 'self' in 2.27.17 is almost identical to the definition of 'person' in 2.27.26 does suggest that we could speak either of the identity of person or of the identity of self. Can we also speak of the difference between man and self as we do of the difference between man and person? In introducing the term 'person', has Locke merely found a new way of talking about the self?

26. Locke expresses this attachment in several ways. We saw above that in 2.27.11 he speaks of the particles of the body being "vitally united" with the "thinking conscious self". We also saw that in 2.27.25 he speaks of "any part of our Bodies vitally united to that which is conscious in us". Such body parts are thereby "a part of our *selves*". In 2.27.27, he tells us that we are ignorant of the "Nature of that thinking thing, that is in us" which we take to be our selves. He goes on to say our lack of knowledge about the self includes not knowing if it is "tied to a certain System of fleeting Animal Spirits". So the self is the thinking thing, the body and its parts are united to the self, and the self is tied to the physiology. The relation of being 'tied to' is left unexplained.

27. The *Education* contains some guidelines for building moral character in children.

28. In 3.11.16, Locke contrasts man in a physical sense with moral man: "And therefore, whether a Child or Changeling be a *Man* in a physical Sense, may amongst the Naturalists be as disputable as it will, it concerns not at all the *moral Man*, as I may call him . . ."

29. The *Oxford English Dictionary* says that 'ingenuous' in the seventeenth century was frequently confused with 'ingenious'. Locke must mean the latter, hence 'skillful' or 'careful' observation of word usage.

30. Cf. 3.11.20 and 3.6.21,22.

31. Reason is an important faculty for Locke. In this passage, he writes as if reason's only function is to understand general signs and make deductions. Elsewhere, he suggests that reason might discover the laws of nature; in the treatise on education, reason becomes the guide of conduct. Reason is also the source of good social relations: God has given

reason "to be the Rule Betwixt Man, and the common body whereby humane kind is united into one fellowship and societie" (*Two Treatises*, 2:172).

32. *Essay* 4.3.23 characterizes man as an "inconsiderable, mean, and impotent a Creature", one of the "lowest of all Intellectual Beings" on the scale of Being.

33. For Locke's discussion of this notion, see, for example, *Essay* 2.31.6,11; 2.32.24; 3.6.3; 4.3.16; 4.3.29; 4.6.11.

34. His precise words are: "the corpuscularian Hypothesis . . . is thought to go farthest in an intelligible Explication of the Qualities of Bodies" (*Essay*, 4.3.16). He goes on to say that "the Weakness of humane Understanding is scarce able to substitute another, which will afford us a fuller and clearer discovery of the necessary Connexion, and *Co-existence*, of the Powers, which are to be observed united in several sorts of them". In his instructions to tutors for science education of young men, Locke suggests that natural philosophy should be studied for the hypotheses advanced, rather than "to understand the Terms and Ways of Talking of the several sects", adding that "the Modern Corpuscularians talk, in most Things, more intelligibly than the Peripateticks" (*Education*, §193).

35. Cf. *Essays on the Law of Nature* where Locke remarks that God has "created the soul and constructed the body with wonderful art, and has thoroughly explored the faculties and powers of each, as well as their hidden constitutions and nature" (p. 155).

36. Locke warns that the knowledge of man acquired from the real essence or the internal constitution would be of little if any use, at least with regard to physical objects. See the microscopical eye example in 2.23.12.

37. Today, we would say that the knowledge of the human genome would yield a detailed knowledge of the sources and causes of many features of humans. An article in the *New York Times* for February 2001 about the human genome project speaks of "the set of DNA-encoded instructions that specify a person". With Locke's distinction between man and person, perhaps we should say the DNA instructions specify a man. Such knowledge derived from that biological source may be the sort of knowledge Locke was suggesting, although hardly a deductive knowledge.

38. When he discusses the chain of being, Locke applies the notion of internal constitution to other members on the chain. He raises the question of whether the "internal Constitution and Frame" of the various creatures on the scale or chain are specifically different, different in kind, remarking that it is impossible for us to say (3.6.22). But he does

say "we have Reason to think, that where the Faculties, or outward Frame so much differs, the internal Constitution is not exactly the same". So the notion of an internal constitution of the Beings or creatures on the chain is clearly entertained. Whatever the internal constitution of non-corporeal Beings might be, it would not be, as with man, an underlying physical structure.

39. See, for example, *Education*, §66.
40. See for example, *Education*, §§101, 102, 122, 126.
41. Ibid., §102.
42. Ibid., §31.
43. Ibid., §41. In the first edition of the *Essay*, Locke refers to "the *Idea* of ourselves, as understanding, rational Creatures" (4.3.18). Subsequent editions replaced 'rational Creatures' with 'rational Beings'. Coste's French translation, made from a later edition, preserves the first edition phrase: "l'idée de Nous-mêmes comme le Créature Intelligent & Raisonnable".
44. *Education*, §81. Cf. "Conduct", §6, p. 26, where he recommends that mathematics "be taught all those who have the time and opportunity, not so much to make them Mathematicians, as to make them reasonable Creatures; for though we all call our selves so, because we are born to it if we please, yet we may truly say Nature gives us but the Seeds of it; we are born to be, if we please, rational Creatures, but 'tis Use and Exercise only that makes us so, and we are indeed so no farther than industry and application has carried us".
45. Ibid. Civilized nations, Locke says later in this work, are "grounded upon Principles of Reason" (§186).
46. *Two Treatises*, 2:27. See section 173: "by Property I must be understood here, as in other places, to mean that Property which Men have in their Person as well as Goods".
47. In *A Dictionary of the English Language*, Samuel Johnson gives the definition as "a possessor in his own right", and then cites the section 44 passage from Locke.
48. Writing about captives taken in a just and lawful war, Locke remarks that the captives are not masters of their own lives. He then continues: "He that is Master of himself, and his own Life, has a right too to the means of preserving it, so that as soon as Compact enters, Slavery ceases" (*Two Treatises*, 2:172).
49. See "Conduct", §43.
50. I qualify this remark about the soul in chapter 5. Once we identify, as does Locke, the soul with one of the spirits on the chain of being, we have to find some way to link the soul and the person at the resurrection.

2. The Universe and Our World

1. That last phrase about happiness merits attention. I discuss it in chapter 3.
2. There is more information concerning Locke's notion of theology in this section of his "Conduct" than just that brief definition. He speaks of theology as a science, one that is "incomparably above all the rest, where it is not by Corruption narrow'd into a Trade or Faction, by mean or ill Ends, and secular Interests" (p. 66). Theology is a "noble Study which is every Man's Duty, and every one that can be call'd a rational Creature is capable of". We get some hint about the relation between knowledge and theology when he explains that "The Works of Nature, and the Words of Revelation, display it [theology] to Mankind in Characters so large and visible, that those who are not quite blind may in them read, and see the first Principles and most necessary Parts of it". That science would "truly enlarge Men's minds". In this brief section of the addendum to the work on human understanding we have a succinct statement of the relation between the *Essay* and the *Reasonableness*.
3. 'World' is sometimes used instead of 'universe', but as we will see, there are other uses of 'world' that are not the same as 'universe'.
4. "Flight controllers at NASA's Jet Propulsion Laboratory reported yesterday that the *Voyagers* show every sign of being able to function long enough for one more significant discovery: the heliopause where the solar system ends and the rest of space begins". An article by John Noble Wilford in the Science Times section of the *New York Times*, Tuesday, August 13, 2002.
5. Perhaps we can say God is part of or in the universe, if Locke agrees with a quotation he cites from Tully concerning 4.10.6: "What can be more silly arrogant and misbecoming than for a man to think he has a Mind and Understanding in him, but yet in all the Universe beside, there is no such thing?"
6. Cf. 2.15.7 on "the Creation, or Fall of the Angels".
7. The notion of 'provinces' has a larger application in Locke's *Education*. He praises Newton for showing us "how far Mathematicks applied to some Parts of Nature, may, upon Principles that Matter of Fact justifie, carry us in the knowledge of some, as I may so call them, particular Provinces of the Incomprehensible Universe" (§194).
8. Natural philosophy and its speculative truth is a branch of science, one of the three sciences Locke distinguishes. There is a possible ambiguity in this remark. Locke is not saying God, Angels and Spirits furnish us with such truths. Rather the study of them, together with the study of bodies (the material world) can lead to such truths. The fact that bodies can be studied with the method of experience and observation,

should not suggest that there are no speculative truths about bodies in the *Essay*. Bodies are the object of experimental science as well as of the enlarged sense of natural philosophy. The same enlarged sense is found in his *Education*, where he identifies two parts to natural philosophy, "one comprehending Spirits with their Nature and Qualities; and the other Bodies". (§190, p. 245 in the Clarendon Edition).

9. See, for example, *Essay* 4.3.24: "we are ignorant of the several Powers, Efficacies, and Ways of Operation, whereby the Effects, which we daily see, are produced". Perhaps the ascription of powers and efficacies to bodies may belong to natural philosophy in the enlarged sense, since those properties are not discoverable by experience and observation.

10. I discuss what he calls an 'extravagant conjecture' in chapter 3.

11. There is one other passage in which Locke identifies a conjecture he made, the notion that morality could be capable of demonstration (4.12.8). When he made that suggestion, he did not speak of conjecture; he was much more positive and confident there (see 3.11.16). In that section he said, "I am bold to think, that *Morality is capable of Demonstration*, as well as Mathematicks".

12. The "Conduct" refers to those who "accustom'd to retir'd Speculations, run natural Philosophy into Metaphysical Notions" (§23).

13. This was not an unusual notion of science. The first edition of the *Encyclopedia Britannica* describes science in philosophy as "any doctrine deduced from self-evident and certain principles". Similarly, Samuel Johnson speaks of science as "certainty grounded on demonstration". Science produces demonstrative knowledge and certainty.

14. *Education*, §190, pp. 244–45. This remark is a bit obscure. The suggestion seems to be that were natural philosophy as a speculative science to be made a proper science, it would eliminate the speculation. 'Reduce' has the sense of ordering or systematizing. In this same section he speaks of a science "that can be methodized into a System". Several passages in the *Essay* speak of 'reduce to rules' (2.28.17 and 4.16.9) and another section refers to reducing an argument to syllogistic form (4.17.4).

15. *Education*, §94, p. 155.

16. Ibid., p. 156.

17. Ibid., §193, p. 247.

18. He rejects this possibility, because he thinks birds have to have ideas as patterns for their songs, and hence a perception of those ideas. A purely material cause is thus rejected. There is no reason to think Locke did not believe that physiology also operates when birds sing. The relation between physiology and birds following the patterns of ideas is not disclosed, nor, of course, does Locke offer an account of that relation when we think and act.

19. For other references to animal spirit physiology in the *Essay*, see: 1.1.2; 2.1.15; 2.8.4,12,21; 2.10.5,10; 2.27.13,27; 2.33.6; 4.10.19.
20. Using a Concordance of the Bible supplied by John Higgins-Biddle, I tracked the references to 'spirits' in the Old and New Testaments. There are not many references. There are a few passages referring to evil spirits, unclean spirits, ministering spirits, and the seven spirits of God. In the Revised Standard Version that I consulted (3rd ed., 1965), some of the references in the Old Testament are translated as 'mediums and wizards'. Of course, there are a great number of passages that refer to the singular form, 'spirit', so perhaps Locke had these references in mind for his history of the Bible for children. Angels are also frequently mentioned.
21. A similar concern is expressed in 2.33.17; the chapter is on the association of ideas. "Intellectual Habits and Defects this way contracted are not less frequent and powerful, though less observed. Let the *Ideas* of Being and Matter be strongly joined either by Education or much Thought, whilst these are still combined in the Mind, what Notions, what Reasonings, will there be about separate Spirits? Let custom from the very Childhood have join'd Figure and Shape to the *Idea* of God, and what Absurdities will that Mind be liable to about the Deity?"
22. The term 'intervention' may be misleading if it suggests special intervention by God as in miracles. Locke defines a miracle as "a sensible Operation, which being above the comprehension of the Spectator, and in his Opinion contrary to the establish'd Course of Nature, is taken by him to be Divine". ('A Discourse of Miracles', in *Posthumous Works*, 1706, p. 217). God as the immaterial cause of gravity is not acting contrary to the established course of nature; it is part of that established course. There was an issue between Leibniz and Samual Clarke over what Leibniz understood as God's constant intervention, according to Newton's account. What we need to recognize is that Locke's appeal to immaterial powers and causes in the *Education* passage is offered as an explanation of an aspect of the ordinary course of nature. Locke does not specify what the actions of immaterial spirits are in our world.
23. See *Reasonableness* in which Locke contrasts the visible world with the intellectual world. "We know little of this visible, and nothing at all of the state of that Intellectual World; wherein are infinite numbers and degrees of Spirits out of the reach of our ken or guess" (pp. 141–42).
24. Locke explains that 'beauty' is a complex idea consisting of several simple ideas, "a certain composition of Colour and Figure, causing delight in the Beholder" (2.12.5; cf. 2.18.4). He also speaks of "the clearness and beauty of a good Stile", the beauty of truth (4.3.20), and in 2.11.2 he associates beauty with wit.

3. The World of God, Angels, and Spirits

1. There is also the well-known comment in which Locke discounts the value of syllogism in reasoning: "But God has not been so sparing to Men to make them barely two-legged Creatures, and left it to *Aristotle* to make them Rational" (4.17.4).
2. For example, *The Reasonableness of Christianity*: the law of reason is a suitable law for "such a Creature as Man, unless God would have made him a Rational Creature, and not required him to have lived by" that law (p. 13; cf. pp. 14, 119, 142). See also pp. 159, 169 for references to 'reasonable Creatures'. The 'Conduct' says "we are born to be, if we please, rational Creatures" (§6, p. 26; see also p. 67 in *Posthumous Works*, 1706). In section 7 of this work, Locke remarks that if we think "That those who have particular Callings" cannot understand mathematics or science, that is not unexpected, but it is proper for us to expect them to "think and reason right about what is their daily employment". If we think them incapable of this, we would level them down with the "Brutes and [we would be] charging them with a Stupidity, below the rank of rational Creatures".
3. What determines the degrees a creature would experience in moving up the chain, or what the states are that they assume, are not specified by Locke. Nor is it clear what creatures would experience these degrees and states. Only humans?
4. The term 'creature' also appears in Locke's 'An Examination of P. Malebranche's Opinion of Seeing All Things in God', in *Posthumous Works*, pp. 146, 167, 175, 191, 208, 212.
5. Some light may be cast on this rather cryptic reference by Locke's comment in this section: "I should remark, that our *Love* and *Hatred* of inanimate insensible Beings, is commonly founded on that Pleasure and Pain which we receive from their use and application any way to our Senses, though with their Destruction". Unclear about this remark is what the Beings are that we love and hate and apply to our senses, resulting in their destruction? The previous section, 2.20.4, spoke of the delight we take in eating grapes. Could that be an example of an inanimate insensible Being? He speaks of inanimate bodies whose characteristic ideas are "Colour, and in some both" color and figure (3.11.19). He also says God has made "the less-excellent pieces of this Universe", that is, inanimate Beings (4.10.12). Another mention of specific inanimate Beings (in this case, bodies) occurs in that curious section about the interrelation of all things. There he cites gold and water. The term 'insensible' has many occurrences (I count 27) but all but two refer to insensible corpuscles or parts of bodies. None of these passages clarifies what the Beings or objects are that we love and hate and destroy. Nor does he say to which senses these Beings are applied.

6. I discuss some of his examples of conceivable and intelligible in chapter 4.
7. He gives the odd example of the first sort as "the clippings of our Beards and pairings of our nails". I would think any bit of matter, even whole objects such as tables and chairs would fit this category.
8. Locke recognized that man is a mixed being, as his label 'corporeal intellectual' clearly indicates. Just how this dual nature works together is not a topic he gives much attention to. But it is clear, I think, that he did not believe thought was a property of the body or brain.
9. Locke's translation in his 'Examination of P. Malebranche's Opinion', p. 204.
10. It is worth recalling that consciousness of our past actions was part of Locke's account of personal identity. The Beings referred to here carry the consciousness of their actions to all their actions. We might say they have perfected the consciousness of their actions and knowledge. Just what actions these Beings perform is left unsaid.
11. The degrees referred to here are different from the 'gentle degrees' that creatures go through as they ascend the scale of being. Only some angels may have larger views and capacities: degrees of angelhood or angelicness?
12. Cf. Berkeley, *Principles*, §81: "That there are a great variety of spirits of different orders and capacities, whose faculties, both in number and extent, are far exceeding those the Author of my being has bestowed on me, I see no reason to deny". He goes on to remark on "the endless variety of spirits and ideas, that might possibly exist."
13. More than that possibility may be beyond our comprehension, although it was not uncommon at that time to speak of minds and souls being in space—not the space of bodies but a different kind of space. He used the term 'expansion' to distinguish it from physical space.
14. Locke contrasts our way of communicating our thoughts with the method used by separate spirits. We must use "corporeal Signs, and particularly Sounds, which are therefore of most general use, as being the best, and quickest we are capable of". Spirits communicate immediately, without signs, but Locke confesses we do not know how this is done (2.23.36). Cf. Pasnau on angel talk (*Thomas Aquinas on Human Nature*, p. 376).
15. He ends *Essay* 2.23.13 with the following remark: "The Supposition at least, that Angels do sometimes assume Bodies, need not startle us, since some of the most ancient, and most learned Fathers of the Church, seemed to believe, that they had Bodies: And this is certain, that their state and way of Existence is unknown to us." Unknown but apparently not beyond conjecture or supposition.
16. Speaking of 'the philosophers', he says that "The chief of their Argu-

ments were from the excellency of Virtue: And the highest they generally went, was the exalting of humane Nature, Whose Perfection lay in virtue" (*Reasonableness*, p. 161). He goes on to describe virtue as "the perfection and excellency of our Nature" (p. 162).

17. Entry on "Pleasure and Pain", printed in von Leyden's edition of *Essays on the Law of Nature*, p. 269.
18. The list of God's properties given in Locke's "Examination of P. Malebranche's Opinion" does not include happiness. "The Ideas of Being, Power, Knowledge, Goodness, Duration, make up the Complex Idea we have" of God and Angels (p. 188).
19. The entry is on pleasure and pain and the passions. It is printed in Von Leyden's edition of the *Essays on the Law of Nature*, p. 269. There is something intriguing about the suggestion that spiritual objects (he does not identify them) can provoke in us "lovely and ravishing thoughts". The contrast with spiritual objects is material objects which "continually importune us".
20. Virtue is the perfection of our nature, happiness our greatest good. Virtue and happiness seem to go together in Locke's account of man.
21. In a section on religion in his "Conduct", Locke says: "Besides his particular Calling for the support of this Life, every one has a concern in a future Life, which he is bound to look after" (§8).
22. Cf. the *Reasonableness* in which he explains that the reward for just men (he refers here to the posterity of Adam) will be "Eternal Life and Bliss" (p. 12; see also pp. 130, 163).
23. Catherine Kemp tells me that this remark is "a precise statement of the common law doctrine of mens rea". She cites a 1551 case of Reniger v. Fogossa: "But where a man breaks the words of the law by involuntary ignorance, there he shall not be excused. As if a person that is drunk kills another, this shall be a felony, and he shall be hanged for it, and yet he did it through ignorance, for when he was drunk he had no understanding nor memory; but inasmuch as that ignorance was occasioned by his own act and folly, and he might have avoided it, he shall not be privileged thereby."

4. Spirits and Our Ideas of Them

1. These early essays identified a fourth kind or source of knowledge, "supernatural and divine revelation, but this is no part of our present argument. For we do not investigate here what a man can experience who is divinely inspired, what a man can behold who is illuminated by a light from heaven" (p. 123). It is fair to say that by the time of the fourth edition of the *Essay*, Locke was rather critical of those enthusiasts who

claimed to be divinely inspired. Whether he thought there were legitimate divine inspirations, I do not know.
2. The same three faculties are invoked in his discussion of our knowledge of the existence of God. "Though GOD has given us no innate *Ideas* of himself; though he has stamped no original Characters on our Minds, wherein we may read his Being: yet having furnished us with those Faculties, our Minds are endowed with, he hath not left himself without witness: since we have Sense, Perception, and Reason, and cannot want a clear proof of him, as long as we carry our selves about us" (*Essay*, 4.10.1).
3. Pasnau's commentary on *Thomas Aquinas on Human Nature* identifies a similar view about the way we form ideas of spirits. "To the extent that we can say something about the alien minds of angels, we do so by looking at our own minds and drawing comparisons". But Pasnau notes that "Reasoning from an analogy between our minds and angelic minds brings limited success" (p. 360). The term 'operations' is rather vague, but I assume the reference is to the operations of the understanding or mind. The notion of attributing all operations to those Beings is misleading. What is attributed to Spirits and God are qualities and powers, along with a select list of properties. Locke is silent on what guides that selection.
4. The *OED* explains that a perch was a rod used to measure land, equal to about five-and-a-half-yards. The original meaning of furlong was "the length of the furrow in the common field", equal to 40 rods or perches.
5. Presumably it is their internal constitution that determines their different degrees, species, and properties. What their internal constitution might be is difficult to imagine.
6. For a discussion of the many uses of this principle of no action at a distance, including cognitive action, see my *Perceptual Acquaintance from Descartes to Reid*, chapter 4.
7. There is an interesting example of what cannot be conceived in the *Essays on the Law of Nature*. Locke was making the point that man is not the maker of himself: "For it cannot be conceived that anything will be so unfriendly, so hostile to itself that, while able to bestow existence on itself, it would not at the same time preserve it, or would willingly let it go, when a little life's brief course had ended; for without it all other precious, useful, agreeable and blessed things cannot be retained and are sought for in vain" (p. 153).
8. Perhaps Locke was referring to some Scholastic source. The notion of species of angels is found in Aquinas; see Pasnau's comment: "We are one of a vast number of species, and though many of these species are part of the corruptible, corporeal world that lies subservient to us, an

even greater number of species rises above us, closer to God" (*Human Nature*, p. 396). Pasnau goes on to say that Aquinas believed in "a vast, vast hierarchy of such kinds of" angels.
9. See *The Library of John Locke*, ed. John Harrison and Peter Laslett (2nd ed., 1971), entry nos. 254, 538.
10. Torvous, stern in aspects; grim, fierce-looking (*OED*).
11. Burthogge's account of spirits fits one of the definitions cited in the *OED*: spirits are "usually regarded as imperceptible at ordinary times to the human senses, but capable of becoming visible at pleasure, and frequently conceived as troublesome, terrifying, or hostile to mankind".
12. For a brief discussion of the reviews of Burthogge's *Essay* in several seventeenth-century journals, see my *Locke and the Way of Ideas*, pp. 20–22. I no longer remember whether the reviews discussed what Burthogge said about spirits. I did suggest that his relative obscurity was "very probably due to the way in which his epistemological discussions were obvious digressions from his main task, i.e. the presentation of a doctrine of a world soul or of the presence of spirits in the world" (p. 21). I went on to say, "His epistemology tended to become lost in these minor theological questions". If this characterization is correct, then we can see how different was Burthogge's discussion of spirits from Locke's. It would be worthwhile for some one to go back and check those reviews to see if there was any account of spirits in them.
13. *The Correspondence of John Locke*, ed. by E. S. De Beer 4:295 (no. 1409). I am indebted to James Buickerood for calling this particular exchange between Locke and Limborch to my attention.
14. *Correspondence*, 4:329 (no. 1428). He may just have used the word 'marvelous' as a descriptive adjective as, "Such as to excite wonder; astonishing, surprising" (*OED*). The *OED* also gives a use in poetry: "Concerned with the supernatural". As a noun it is "that which is prodigious, and extravagantly improbable".
15. See letter no. 1447, dated 12/22 January 1692. For the full details on the opposition to Bekker's book, see Andrew Fix, *Fallen Angels: Balthasar Bekker, Spirit Belief, and Confessionalism in the Seventeenth Century Dutch Republic*, pp. 75–79, as well as chapter 5.
16. Bekker, vol. 2, ch. 1, §10, p. 14. Each volume contains one of the four books of *Le monde enchanté*.
17. Ibid., §11, p. 15.
18. Ibid., §17, p. 21; ch. 2 §1, p. 23; ch. 4 §1, p. 57.
19. Ch. 4, §2, p. 58.
20. One curiosity is Bekker's use of the same talking parrot story used by Locke. See vol. 4, ch. 7, pp. 120–28. The title of this chapter announces that he will examine what has been said about a certain bird that spoke like a human because, it was thought, the devil had caused it to do so.

Far from the devil instructing the parrot, Bekker describes ways in which by signs and gestures birds can be taught to imitate speech. Bekker has some useful remarks on this topic. Locke's use of the story about the parrot was quite different.

21. See volume 1, ch. 20, especially §§2–11, pp. 270–90. Also the whole of chapter 20. The chapters cover the beliefs of Christians. For that, Bekker seems to rely upon the account given by Caspar Schott in his *Physica curiosa* (1662). Bekker says that it is this book and another by the same author (*Magia Universalis, la Magie Universelle*) on which he has relied. He works to debunk all these beliefs.
22. Vol. 2, ch. 1, §16, p. 21.
23. Ch. 3, §6, p. 47,
24. Ibid., §8, pp. 49–50.
25. Ibid., §8, p. 51. I suspect this cognitive concept of place was missed by Bekker's critics in Holland. One of his most vociferous critics, Fix tells us, was Everhardus van der Hooght who argued that "It was also clear from the Bible that spirits could be in a place. . . . Scripture often said that Spirits moved from one place to another" (*Fallen Angels*, p. 85).
26. "Balthasar Bekker's Cartesian Hermeneutics and the Challenge of Spinozism", *British Journal for the History of Philosophy* 1:1 (1993), 61.
27. *Correspondence*, 4:296 (no. 1409), dated 21/31 July 1691. I do not think it is at all clear that the soul acts on its body. If, as it seems, the soul's actions are only cognitive, the relation between the soul and its body would not seem to cause the body to move. The soul does the thinking for the man, but that would not be an action on the body. It might be an action that occurs with the body, in conjunction with the physiology.
28. "Angels, Devils, and Evil Spirits in Seventeenth-Century Thought: Balthasar Bekker and the Collegiants", *Journal of the History of Ideas* 50, no. 1 (1989): 536.
29. I have obviously not gone into a detailed analysis even of volume 2 of this prolix work. There may be other aspects worth attention in his account of spirits, or his appeal to experience in his negative critique of them and the various beliefs about them, or his interpretation of Scriptures on these topics. But it is clear that there is nothing like the account of spirits found in Locke nor, I suspect, would Locke's acceptance of separate spirits with the soul as one of them come under Bekker's concern.

5. Souls That Become Spirits

1. Locke's Dutch friend, Limborch, also rejected that Cartesian notion. In his account of Bekker's claims, Limborch said Bekker had an inade-

quate concept of soul. Limborch then went on to say: "That thought is essential to spirit I would certainly not call in question; whether, however, the nature of spirit requires that it should always be thinking in action I do not determine; much less, that there is nothing in spirit except thought pure and simple. That our soul acts upon our body and in turn our body upon our soul is evident from experience; that this reciprocal action can be explained through the bare ideas of thought and extension is something that the followers of Descartes have not yet taught us (*The Correspondence of John Locke*, vol. 4, no. 1409, July 1691: 296–97).

2. For some discussion of the soul in the *Essay*, see my *A Locke Dictionary*, the entry for 'soul'.
3. The phrase 'real Being' might be thought to contrast with 'unreal' or 'imaginary Beings', but I do not think Locke ever refers to imaginary Beings. 'Real Being' may just be a way of stressing the 'beingness' of the soul. The soul is not a quality, relation, or mode. It is substance-like in the sense that it is the subject of qualities, powers, and functions. The creatures, Beings, angels and spirits I discussed in chapter 3 are all real Beings, although Locke does not describe them in that way. There seems to be no difference between a Being and a real Being. A comparison might be made with another frequently used phrase, 'real existence', which is often paired with just 'existence'. 'Real' in both usages is an 'emphasis' word.
4. Locke's commentary on Malebranche's talk of God 'penetrating' the mind moves between God penetrating our mind, soul or spirit. (See his *Examination of P. Malebranche's Opinion*, p. 187).
5. See *Reasonableness*, p. 163: "'Twill be idle for us, who know not how our own Spirits move, and act us, to ask in what manner the Spirit of God shall work".
6. The interplay between the soul and the man may reflect some tensions and difficulties in scholastic (at least, Thomistic) accounts. Reading Robert Pasnau's recent book, *Thomas Aquinas on Human Nature* (2002), I was struck by the similarity of a number of themes in Pasnau's commentary to those I have found in Locke concerning the relation of man, person, soul, and body. Of particular interest is the discussion of the individuation of souls and the question of whether a soul that leaves the body is the same soul that was attached to the body. See Pasnau's chapter 12, "Life After Death", with its sections on separated souls and identity and resurrection (pp. 361–93).
7. 'The Spirits of just Men made perfect' is found in the New Testament: Hebrews, 12.23.
8. It is useful to remind ourselves that the chain of being is a metaphor. To speak of going up the chain, or of being located higher on the chain

translates into more reality, greater perfection, more knowledge, perhaps also greater value or importance.

9. This section considers the possibility of "the same Person [appearing] at the Resurrection, though in a Body not exactly in make or parts the same which he has here" (2.27.15).

10. Etienne Balibar has a nice phrase for linking personal identity to responsibility: "le critère de l'identité (et donc de l'imputabilité et de la responsabilité des actes", *Identité et différence,* p. 242.

11. For a fine discussion of this point, see Balibar, entry for 'Resurrection'.

12. I assume that 'finite Spirits' includes all the spirits on the chain of being. Do they all have a place?

13. If thoughts and the operations of the mind or soul, which are not Beings, have a beginning, does existence also determine them? The passage in §3 seems limited to Beings.

14. There is one exception to the stress on a specific shape. See the discussion of the misshapen Bishop, *Essay,* 3.6.26. In this case, rationality and immaterial spirit turn out to be more important.

15. The sentence went on to explain that a few difficulties were not a sufficient reason for doubting the existence of spirits, just as "because the notion of body is cumbred with some difficulties very hard, and, perhaps, impossible to be explained, or understood by us" is sufficient to doubt their existence (2.23.31). He continues: "For I would fain have instanced any thing in our notion of Spirit more perplexed, or nearer a Contradiction, than the very notion of Body includes in it; the divisibility in infinitum of any finite Extension, involving us, whether we grant or deny it, in consequences impossible to be explicated, or made in our apprehensions consistent; Consequences that carry greater difficulty, and more apparent absurdity, than any thing can follow from the Notion of an immaterial knowing substance".

16. Are other spirits among the ranks also able to enjoy eternal duration? Or is this a condition reserved for human souls? John Higgins-Biddle has pointed out to me that there is a difference between being eternal and being created but able to enjoy eternal life.

17. Explicating Corinthians 6.9, Locke says: "no one who is unrighteous, i.e. comes short of perfect Righteousness, shall be admitted into the Eternal Life of that Kingdom", that is "the Heavenly Kingdom of the Messiah" (*Reasonableness,* p. 117). Another remark is even more relevant: "Righteousness, or Compleat Obedience [to the laws of that Kingdom], did thus Justifie, or make them Just, and thereby capable of Eternal Life" (p. 118; cf. p. 12). The issue of whether justification is by faith or by works, deeds done in this life, is apparently involved in the notion of the just man and who merits, and for what reason, eternal life.

Locke presents both sides of the issue in *Reasonableness*. Essay 4.17.13 also reflects that issue. The question is, does God make a man just as well as judge him to have been just? At the very least, I would think the judgment is made on the basis of how a man has performed in this life. Hence, Locke's great concern for morality and virtue. Whether this means Locke came down on the side of works rather than faith alone for justification, I leave for others to decide. That the issue is found in the *Essay* is another indication of the theological undercurrent in that work. For his discussion of the issue, see his *Reasonableness*, especially chapters 3 and 11.

18. There is a curious remark in Locke's *Paraphrases of St. Paul's Epistles*, commenting on Paul's letter to the Corinthians (1 Cor. 15), in which he distinguishes between earthly and heavenly bodies: "those who are raised to an heavenly state shall have other Bodys", and those heavenly bodies will be beautiful and excellent, "of a very different constitution and qualitys from those they had before" (p. 252). It is again interesting to find Locke ascribing beauty to features of that intellectual world. What the beauty would be of those heavenly bodies is not clear, nor can we easily determine why a heavenly body is still a body. For some brief discussion of this remark, see my *A Locke Dictionary*, entry for 'resurrection'. In chapter 11 of *Reasonableness*, Locke explains the phrase, 'Redemption of our Body', as "Whereby is plainly meant the change of these frail Mortal Bodies, into the Spiritual Immortal Bodies at the Resurrection" (p. 115). In the Revised Standard Edition of the Bible, Corinthians 1.15.40 reads: "There are celestial bodies and there are terrestrial bodies; but the glory of the celestial is one, and the glory of the terrestrial is another"; 1 Cor. 15.44 reads: "It is sown a physical body, it is raised a spiritual body". This may have been a common conception at the time. Andrew Fix ("Angels, Devils, and Evil Spirits in Seventeenth-Century Thought: Balthasar Bekker and the Collegiants") cites one of the Dutch Collegiants, Lambert Joosten, who apparently claimed that angels were creatures with 'fine spiritual bodies, like God'. Joosten maintained that angels 'are created by God and exist in their own way and of another rank than men, having no flesh or bones, but bodies of very fine material' (p. 546).

19. The emotionally charged criticism of bodily shape in *Essay* 4.4.15 is directed against a body of material, physical shape, not against heavenly bodies or heavenly shape. There is no suggestion in the *Essay* that the bodily form at the resurrection will be non-material. Locke apparently accepted the resurrection of the body, that traditional doctrine. Would a transformation of the earthly body into a heavenly one count as the resurrection of the earthly body? Is it the case that the souls of men that become spirits on the chain of being and enjoy eternal life,

bliss, and happiness require bodies of some sort, while angels and other spirits do not need bodies?
20. The notion of a mass of matter (i.e. the body) being restored to such a state sounds a bit odd, but this remark is part of his polemic against saying it is the human shape of that mass of matter that warrants eternal life. It is of course the nature of the life lived by the man that is important.
21. For a discussion of this question, see chapter 3 of my *Realism and Appearances*.

6. General Conclusion

1. Unfortunately he did not give us a list of speculative sciences. We can say that natural philosophy in Locke's enlarged sense is one, but what others are there?
2. Cf. Balibar, p. 241: "La question du Jugement Dernier et celle de la Résurrection, étroitement liées entre elles, occupent une place remarquable dans le Traité de Locke". The 'Traité' is his way of describing *Essay* 2.27, the chapter on identity and diversity. He has in mind sections 15, 20, 22, and 26.
3. For further discussion of these various Kingdoms, see the *Reasonableness*, pp. 38, 66, 89–90, 97, 116–17.

BIBLIOGRAPHY

Balibar, Etienne. *Identité et différence: l'invention de la conscience. An Essay concerning Human Understanding, II, xvii; Of Identity and Diversity; l'invention de la conscience.* Présenté, traduit et commenté. Paris: Editions du Seuil, 1998.

Bekker, Balthasar. *Le Monde Enchanté, ou examen des communs sentimens touchant les Esprits, leur nature, leurs pouvoir, leur administration, & leur opérations. Et touchant les éfets que les hommes sont capables de produire par leur communication & leur vertue.* 4 vols. Amsterdam: Chez Pierre Rotterdam, Libraire sur le Vygendam, 1694. (The copy we have has a fifth volume, carrying Bekker's title on the binding and 'vol v' at the bottom of each gathering. See Binet.)

Binet, Benjamin. *Traité Historique des Dieux et des Demons du Paganisme. Avec quelques remarques critiques sur le systême de Mr. Bekker.* Delff: Chez André Voorstad, Marchand Librarie proche la Maison de Ville, 1696. Alexandre Cioranescu in *Bibliographie de la littérature française du dix-septième siècle* lists Binet's book without any mention of its being printed as volume 5 of Bekker. I can only assume there were two different printings, one separate, the other as part of Bekker's *Le monde enchanté*. Binet also published another attack on Bekker in 1699.

Bunge, Wiep van. "Balthasar Bekker's Cartesian Hermeneutics and the Challenge of Spinozism". *Journal of the History of Philosophy* 1 (1993): 55–79.

Fix, Andrew. "Angels, Devils, and Evil Spirits in Seventeenth-Century Thought: Balthasar Bekker and the Collegiants", *Journal of the History of Ideas* 50 (1989): 527–47.

——. "Balthasar Bekker and the Crisis of Cartesianism". *History of European Ideas* 17 (1993): 575–88.
——. *Fallen Angels. Bathasar Bekker, Spirit Belief, and Confessionalism and the Seventeeth Century Dutch Republic.* Dordrecht, Boston: Kluwer Academic, 1999.
Harrison, John, and Peter Laslett. *The Library of John Locke.* 2d ed. Oxford: Clarendon Press, 1971.
Jolley, Nicholas. *Locke: His Philosophical Thought.* Oxford: Oxford University Press, 1999.
Lowe, E. J. *Subjects of Experience.* Cambridge: Cambridge University Press, 1996.
Parmentier, Marc. *Introduction à l'Essai sur l'entendement humain de Locke.* Paris: Presses Universitaires de France, 1999.
Pasnau, Robert. *Thomas Aquinas on Human Nature. A Philosophical Study of Summa theologiae 1a 75–89.* Cambridge: Cambridge University Press, 2003.
Yolton, John W. *A Locke Dictionary.* Oxford: Blackwell, 1993.
——. *Perceptual Acquaintance from Descartes to Reid.* Minneapolis: University of Minnesota Press, 1984.
——. *Realism and Appearances: An Essay in Ontology.* Cambridge: Cambridge University Press, 2000.

INDEX

actions, 6, 19, 69
  and agency, 14
  agent of, 8
  cognitive, 143
  moral, 8, 17, 24, 64, 136
Adam
  his fall, 148, 165
angels, 4, 7, 47, 87, 97, 107, 113, 117, 135, 141, 164
  degrees of, 5 (*see also* species)
  fall of, 72, 160
  good and bad, 110–111
  their spiritual bodies, 172
  their superior knowledge, 121, 137
animals, 26, 33, 41, 52, 54, 65, 66, 88, 90, 107, 119, 123, 128, 149
animal spirits, 57, 125, 154, 156, 162
apparitions, 106, 107
Aquinas, Thomas, 164, 166, 167, 169
Aristotle, 163
atheism, 109

Balibar, Etienne, 8, 154, 155, 156, 170, 172
beasts, 38, 66
beauty, 60–61, 90, 139, 150, 162, 171
Beer, E. S. de, 167
Bekker, Balthasar, 106, 108–112, 142, 167, 168, 171
belief, 51, 115, 124, 151, 168
Bible, 105, 162, 168
  spirits in, 59
birds
  cause of their singing, 57
  their ideas as patterns, 161
bliss, 85, 134, 142, 148, 165, 172

bodies
  celestial, 171
  corpuscular structure of, 9, 32, 74
  physical, 147
  spiritual, 108, 133, 147
Boyle, Robert, 51, 137
brain
  events, 10
  impressions on, 12
  and nerves, 19, 88
  relation to the mind, 134
  role in thinking and perceiving, 143
  states, 11
  thought as one of its properties, 17, 102, 164
  traces, 12
Buickerood, James G., 167
Bunge, Wiep van, 111
Burthogge, Richard, 106–108, 141–142, 167

Carolina
  Constitutions of the, 35
Cartesian, 12, 84, 168 (*see also* Descartes, René)
cause, 58, 155
  of a bird's singing, 57
  and body, 104
  of sensible ideas, 103
certainty, 51, 103, 161
chain of Being, 59, 62, 66, 89, 113, 117, 126, 139, 140, 142, 147, 149, 152, 158, 164,
  creatures and Beings above us, 65, 68, 70, 91
  man's location on, 38

chain of Being (continued)
  as a metaphor, 148, 150, 1169–170
  the soul as one of the spirits
chance, 85, 146
changelings, 66, 132, 156
children, 31, 52, 93, 106, 107, 137, 146, 153, 156
Christian
  beliefs, 151
  doctrine, 142, 150
Christianity, 38
Christians, 85, 109, 110, 111, 112, 145, 168
Clarke, Samuel, 162
conceiving, 8, 69, 98–105
Conduct of the Understanding, 35, 38, 39, 50, 60, 61, 72, 83, 144, 146, 153, 155, 159, 160, 161, 163, 165
conjectures, 3, 49, 51–53, 52, 53, 57, 74–77, 88, 133, 135, 136, 137, 138, 139, 140, 164
consciousness
  cognitive, 22
  moral, 22, 24
  of past actions, 16, 20, 22, 23, 87, 132, 135, 142, 164
  as a property of the brain, 12
  relation to the person, 14, 23, 87, 122, 125, 129
  and the self, 18, 19
corpuscular theory, 28
Coste, Pierre, 158
creatures, 1, 8, 26, 27, 38, 39, 43, 65–68, 88, 90, 99, 110, 114, 140, 149, 151, 169
  biological, 33
  intellectual, 67
  ranks of, 52
  rational, 14, 31–32, 35, 144–145, 159, 163
  species of, 67
  two-legged, 163
Cudworth, Ralph, 106

demons, 110
  evil, 109
demonstration, 5, 51, 54, 161
  mathematical, 144
Descartes, René, 21, 130, 169
devils, 107, 108, 109, 111, 112, 113, 147, 167, 168

domain(s)
  of God, Angels and Spirits, 39, 43, 61, 64, 88, 89, 90, 101, 105, 140, 147, 149
  immaterial, 64
  material, 1, 62, 65
  physical, 16
  spiritual, 1
  theological, 38
dualism
  property, 12, 13, 154
  substance, 11, 12
duration, 68, 72, 79, 80, 93, 95, 96, 102, 103, 104, 113
  eternal, 99
  of God, 103
  infinite, 98

education, 9, 145, 162
England, 111, 114
Essays on the Law of Nature, 3, 47, 91, 138–141, 140, 158, 166
essence, 55, 81
  God's, 79
  nominal, 26, 28, 53
  real, 26, 27, 28, 30, 55, 56, 66, 79, 151, 158
  traditional doctrine of, 66
eternity, 85, 95, 96, 98
  filled by God, 99
ethics, 16, 46, 61
expansion, 94, 98, 104, 164
experience, 8, 29, 78, 92, 129, 135, 168
  and observation, 31, 33, 47, 48, 53, 55, 70, 115, 136, 137, 138, 160, 161
experiments, 52, 146
extension, 68, 98, 101, 169

faculties, 5, 28, 30, 36, 59, 65, 71, 97, 133, 159, 166
  cognitive, 107, 137
  mental, 8
  of the mind, 113, 143, 155
  of other intelligent Beings, 87
  of the soul, 114, 115, 116
  of spirits, 72, 77, 141, 164
Filmer, Robert, 35, 67
Fix, Andrew, 112, 167, 168, 171
freedom, 15, 34, 59, 64

genome
  human, 150, 158
ghosts, 106, 112
goblins, 106, 107
God, 7, 16, 27, 38, 39, 54, 58, 62, 65, 68, 70, 74, 75, 84, 128
  as an agent, 16
  his design, 78
  and eternity, 95
  existence of, 8, 156, 166
  idea of, 3, 94, 96, 97, 162, 165
  his knowledge, 93, 137
  part of the universe, 160
  as pure spirit, 119
  spirit of, 105
gravity, 58, 162
  immaterial cause of, 106
guess, 136, 139, 140

happiness, 8, 22, 23, 24, 33, 45, 79, 88, 98, 134, 145, 147, 149, 156, 160, 172
  degrees of, 90
  the end of man, 82–86
  eternal, 83, 144
  of God and angels, 79–82, 139
  infinite, 142
  of mankind, 39, 83
  in the next life, 2
  perfect, 72
  of spirits, 52, 82
Harrison, John, 167
heaven, 107, 165
Higgins-Biddle, John, 162
Holland, 110, 111, 112, 168
Hooght, Everhardus van der, 168
Hume, David, 137
hypotheses, 57, 158

immateriality, 89, 114, 152
  of the soul, 151
immortality, 1, 13, 36, 38, 63, 85, 114, 118, 120, 130–134, 132, 133, 148, 151, 152, 142 147
  of the soul, 135, 150
innate, 84, 138
  ideas, 151, 153
  ideas of God, 2, 3, 5
  moral rules, 101, 102
  principles, 2, 4, 6, 30
  truths, 30
intentions, 16, 17, 25, 125

Jesus, 148
Johnson, Samuel, 159, 161
Jolley, Nicholas, 11, 154
Joosten, Lambert, 171
justice, 101, 131
  divine, 85

Kant, I., 10, 134, 154
Kemp, Catherine, 165
Kingdom of God, 3, 85, 147, 148
Kingdom of Heaven, 148, 152
Kingdom of the Messiah, 3, 148, 170
knowledge, 4, 16, 27, 33, 49, 51, 79, 92, 93, 102, 146
  beginnings of, 4
  certain, 55, 113
  of God, 38
  imperfections of, 4
  intuitive, 121
  limitations of, 1, 113

Laslett, Peter, 167
law, 87, 102
  of nature, 68
  of reason, 163
laws, 22, 26
  God's, 37, 151
  human, 153
  moral, 16, 84, 138
  of nature, 16, 17, 34, 37, 156
Leibniz, G. W., 162
Leyden, W. von, 165
liberty, 6, 14, 15, 16, 67, 69, 81, 82
life
  eternal, 147, 165, 170, 171
Limborch, Philippus van, 108–111, 167, 168, 169
London, 100, 111, 143
Lowe, E. J., 17, 155, 156

magic, 112
Malebranche, P., 59, 71, 103, 131, 169
materialism, 9, 11, 12, 13, 14, 17, 61, 70, 105, 152
mathematics, 57, 159, 160, 161
matter, 95, 107, 119, 132, 172
  of bodies, 74
  corpuscular particles of, 36
  corpuscular structure of, 27, 29, 133
  corpuscular theory of, 58, 136
  inner constitution, 133

matter (continued)
  masses of, 43, 44
  particles of, 13, 25, 29, 32, 48, 96, 122, 128
  refined, 107
  structure of, 8, 28
  of the universe, 42
maxims, 4, 55
memory, 5, 12, 31, 72, 94, 113, 153
metaphysics, 54, 56, 57, 161
microscope, 75
microscopical eyes, 76, 158
mind, 16, 25, 31, 113, 116, 138
  and body, 9, 36, 134, 139, 151
  faculties of, 5
  powers of, 15
  and soul, 10
miracles, 162
misery, 22, 23, 33, 83, 84, 144, 147, 155
mixed modes, 7, 32, 65, 78
morality, 126, 145, 147, 161, 171
More, Henry, 106

natural philosophy, 46–51, 53, 54–58, 113, 137, 138, 158, 160, 161, 172
Newton, Isaac, 162
New York Times, 158, 160
Noah, 58
  and the flood, 23

observation, 47, 146
ontology, 10, 11, 118, 130, 151
Orchard, N., 110
Oxford, 100, 143

Paley, William, 86
Paris, 111
Parmentier, Marc, 22, 155, 156
parrot, talking, 129
Pascal, B., 5, 94
Pasnau, Robert, 164, 166, 167, 169
Paul, Saint, 171
perceiving, 10, 18, 19
perception, 30, 43, 45, 52, 74, 102, 115, 116, 132, 166
  causal explication of, 12
  conscious, 11
  sense, 3, 91, 133, 145
perfection, 77–79, 88, 121, 165, 170
  degrees of, 90, 149
  of knowledge, 86
  in knowledge and happiness, 150

person
  moral, 31
  as moral agent, 23
  name of self, 19, 20, 21, 22, 34
personality, 86, 87, 88, 120
physiology, 39, 57, 77, 113, 131, 134, 143, 162, 168
place, 143, 168
pleasure, 30, 79, 80, 82, 91, 97, 155
  intellectual, 80
  and pain, 84, 163, 165
power, 9, 14, 15, 16, 17, 25, 28, 42, 69, 71, 79, 80, 82, 92, 105, 155, 169
  causal, 133
  of God, 66
  immaterial, 58–59, 162
  of spirits, 72, 107, 118
principles
  immaterial, 58, 59
  innate, 115
  moral, 101, 104
  theological, 95
probability, 51
proof(s), 78, 145
  of spirits, 153
properties, 30, 41, 52, 66, 78, 81
  of body, 17
  God's, 165
  immaterial, 155
  moral, 39
  neural, 17
  neurobiological, 14
  of spirits, 140
property, 34, 159
provinces, 45, 46, 60, 136, 160

qualities, 92, 169
  of bodies, 158
  experienced, 91
  observed, 33
  of spirits, 161
  primary and secondary, 32, 98
  sensible, 130

rationality, 9, 14, 16, 17, 27, 31, 33, 136, 138, 145
reason, 5, 21, 66, 91, 138, 139, 145, 156, 166
  faculty of, 31
  in making discoveries, 3
The Reasonableness of Christianity, 3,

78, 83, 85, 145, 146, 147, 148, 150, 153, 160, 162, 163, 165, 169, 170, 171, 172
reflection, 93, 139, 140
religion, 75, 86, 109, 113, 144, 145, 147, 150, 165
resurrection, 15, 36, 62, 89, 101, 123, 125, 132, 133, 139, 142, 147, 148, 150, 151, 152, 159, 170, 171
revelation, 62, 104, 105, 160

Schott, Caspar, 168
science(s), 7, 55, 152, 160
  of bodies, 113
  deductive, 27, 30, 75
  demonstrative, 55
  divisions of, 1, 45
  education, 56
  experimental, 27, 29, 47, 50, 52, 70, 113, 137, 138, 161
  of man, 137
  moral, 139
  a priori, 47, 92, 113, 137
  speculative, 56, 137, 139, 161, 172
sensation, 5, 31, 45, 57, 74, 93, 140, 156
sense, 139, 166
signs, 25, 26, 45, 46, 72, 77, 156, 168
  doctrine of, 64
Socrates, 123, 156
Some Thoughts concerning Education, 30, 31, 32, 35, 39, 59, 60, 61, 63, 106, 117, 154, 156, 158, 159, 160, 161, 162
soul, 7, 36, 54, 59, 62, 63, 69, 90, 147, 158
  capable of motion, 100
  as a real Being, 89, 100, 117, 143, 148
  at the resurrection, 152, 159
  as spirit, 8, 110, 114–135, 153
space, 41, 68, 72, 94, 98, 113, 160, 164
  empty, 105
  imaginary, 42
species, 53, 56, 65, 66, 67, 108, 119, 149, 166
  of angels, 70, 97, 107, 166
  of intelligent creatures, 120
spectres, 106, 107
speculation, 2, 49, 51, 52, 57, 61, 62, 137, 138, 161

spirit
  immaterial, 122, 127, 129, 170
  Mosaical, 106
  rational, 127
spirits, 2, 3, 4, 46, 49, 54, 58, 60, 62, 63, 70–73, 88, 91–93, 135, 137, 139, 141, 166
  animal, 12, 25, 57
  cited in the Bible, 162
  created, 119
  evil, 112, 168
  finite, 128
  ideas of, 3
  immaterial, 162
  proof of, 2
  ranks of, 72, 77, 82, 94, 119, 131
  separate, 2, 3, 72, 79, 117, 142, 151, 162, 164, 168
  species of, 86
  their motion, 99
  unclean, 162
sprights, 107
Stillingfleet, E., Bishop of Worcester, 12, 124, 125
Strasbourg
  clock of, 29
substance, 17, 18, 20, 40, 41, 69, 78, 92, 103, 108, 129
  complete, 21
  extended, 25
  identity and diversity of, 19
  immaterial, 11, 13, 20, 114, 123, 124, 154, 155, 170
  material, 17
  physical, 33
  psychological, 17, 21
superstitions, 106
supposition, 72, 125, 135, 136, 137, 140, 164
Sydenham, Thomas, 51, 137

theology, 2, 8, 38, 39, 63, 80, 109, 134, 144, 148, 150, 151, 160, 167, 171
thinking matter, 11, 12, 43, 70
time, 42, 44, 95, 99
truth, 55, 115, 121, 136, 138, 153, 162
  conceptual, 103
  empirical, 46, 51
  infallible, 102
  speculative, 46, 47, 51
Two Treatises of Government, 17, 35, 39, 67, 153, 158, 159

uneasiness, 6, 83, 84
universe, 1, 7, 8, 38, 40–45, 64, 68, 70, 75, 88, 93, 94, 97, 106, 141, 150, 160, 163
   mansions of, 149
   parts of, 65

virtue, 5, 6, 9, 24, 31, 86, 152, 155, 165, 171

Wilford, John Noble, 160
witchcraft, 112
witches, 106, 112
wizards, 106, 162

world, 72, 98
   end of, 71
   of God, Angels and Spirits, 2, 51, 86
   intellectual, 2, 3, 40, 45, 48, 59–62, 82, 87, 88, 90, 134, 135, 136, 141, 147, 148, 162, 171
   material, 1, 48, 49, 50, 51, 64, 136, 160
   next, 85, 86
   physical, 136, 152, 155
   sensible, 48, 49
   visible, 48